D1414140

SUBVERTING THE POWER OF PREJUDICE

Resources for Individual and Social Change

SANDRA L. BARNES

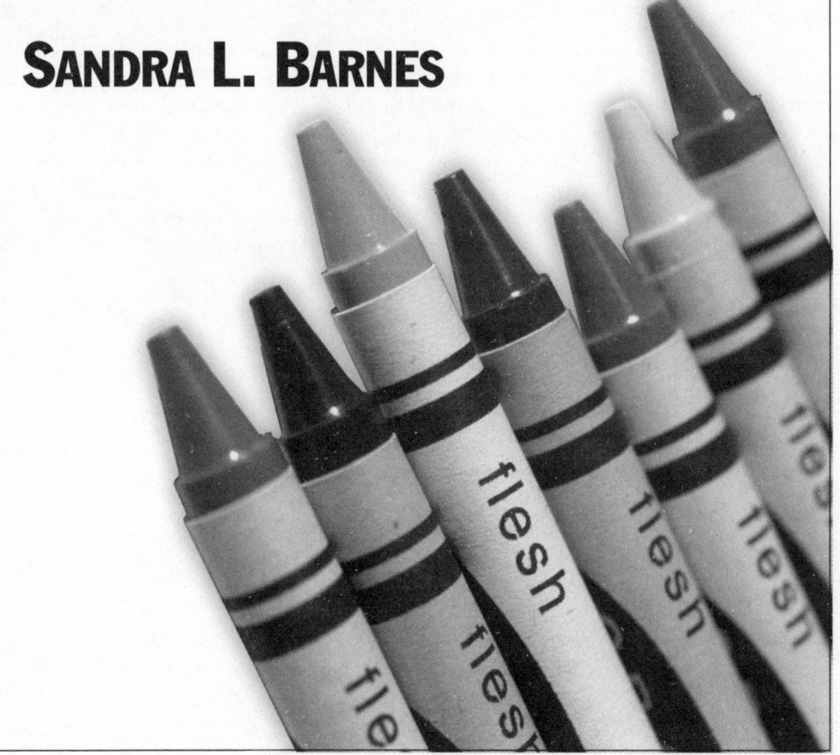

An imprint of InterVarsity Press
Downers Grove, Illinois

InterVarsity Press
P.O. Box 1400, Downers Grove, IL 60515-1426
World Wide Web: www.ivpress.com
E-mail: mail@ivpress.com

InterVarsity Press® is the book-publishing division of InterVarsity Christian Fellowship/USA®, a student movement active on campus at hundreds of universities, colleges and schools of nursing in the United States of America, and a member movement of the International Fellowship of Evangelical Students.
For information about local and regional activities, write Public Relations Dept., InterVarsity Christian Fellowship/USA, 6400 Schroeder Rd., P.O. Box 7895, Madison, WI 53707-7895, or visit the IVCF website at <www.intervarsity.org>.

Design: Cindy Kiple

Images: David Mcglynn/GettyImages

ISBN-10: 0-8308-3339-0
ISBN-13: 978-0-8308-3339-9

Printed in the United States of America ∞

Library of Congress Cataloging-in-Publication Data

Barnes, Sandra L.
Subverting the power of prejudice: resources for individual and social
change/Sandra L. Barnes.
p. cm.
Includes bibliographical references and index.
ISBN-13: 978-0-8308-3339-9 (pbk.: alk. paper)
ISBN-10: 0-8308-3339-0 (pbk.: alk. paper)
1. Discrimination—Religious aspects—Christianity. 2.
1. Title.
BT745.B37 2006
241'.675—dc22

2005033145

P *18 17 16 15 14 13 12 11 10 9 8 7 6 5 4 3 2 1*
Y *20 19 18 17 16 15 14 13 12 11 10 09 08 07 06*

Contents

Introduction

PREPARING FOR BATTLE

An unstated rule of conversation is to avoid discussions about potentially sensitive subjects such as politics, religion and sex because they can result in passion-filled, heated dialogue. I would like to add another topic to this forbidden list: *prejudices.[1] This topic is not easy to discuss because it can result in emotionally intense conversations—often based on personal experiences. To honestly address prejudices requires asking and answering difficult, often uncomfortable questions. The idea that a person can be treated unequally or thought about in disparaging ways based on *ethnicity, *religion, *sex, *creed, *social status, *gender, *physical appearance, ethnicity, sexual orientation, *race, age or national origin can make the most level-headed person angry, despondent or depressed. Most people have experienced prejudice in some form. Some persons believe that their lives have been shaped and their destinies determined by it. Others deny its very existence (Gaertner and Dovidio 1986). However sensitive, it is incumbent upon our society, especially the Christian community, to proactively examine and address the issue of prejudices. Lately we have witnessed an increase of interpersonal and group conflict in the form of terrorism, sexual harassment accusations, race riots, hate crimes and anti-Semitism. Seminars, discussion groups, forums are sponsored, even legislation enacted in an attempt to find so-

---

[1]Words marked with asterisks appear in the glossary at the end of the book.

lutions to such dilemmas. However, I contend that fewer people are seeking answers and direction from the Word of God.

This book addresses the issue of prejudices from the perspectives of those who harbor prejudices and those who experience them. Although I will provide detailed definitions of this concept in subsequent chapters, a basic definition of prejudice is in order here. Prejudice is generally defined in sociology as rigid, illogical, incorrect ideas, thoughts, beliefs and feelings about others. Prejudices are attitudes (i.e., they exist in our minds). But sometimes prejudices can influence our behavior—such actions are often referred to as *discrimination. Thus discrimination reflects behavior—what we say or do (and in some cases, what we fail to say or do). As I will examine in subsequent chapters, research suggests that prejudices and discrimination are often correlated. So although this book focuses on prejudices (attitudes, beliefs, ideas and thoughts), I also consider the implications of discrimination. Prejudices can also result in nondiscriminatory outcomes that do not parallel a Christian stance—avoidance behavior, ambivalence, *stereotypes, anger, misplaced fear and blame—to name a few. This book discusses prejudices and their possible side effects and provides biblical as well as sociological guidelines to help identify areas where individual growth is needed. I also provide information for collective action such that readers will be encouraged to become informed about and engaged in group-level programs to address societal prejudices.

The primary goal of this book is to examine the twofold dimension of prejudice and its effect on the lives of Christians. A prejudicial experience involves two parties: the bearer of the prejudice and the receiver of the prejudice. Let's consider a basic example. Bob harbors prejudicial views about Tom. In this scenario, Bob is the bearer of the prejudice and Tom is the recipient of the prejudice—meaning Bob's thoughts serve to perpetuate prejudice and Tom experiences its effects (sometimes directly, other times indirectly). I examine prejudices from the perspective of two concepts: *power and *peace. Rather than reflecting a particular Christian tradition or religious perspective (for example, Pentecostal, Holiness, Fundamentalist),[2] I link these two points of reference to *inten-*

---

[2]Readers should also note the value in understanding different Christian perspectives as another possible tool to reduce possible prejudices.

tionality that Christians, in general, are challenged to possess.

In this book the concept of *power* refers to the ability or wherewithal that enables Christians to think, feel and behave in godly ways that parallel those in the life of Jesus Christ. This ability is divine in origin (Acts 1:8), but reflects a desire to *choose* to use it in order to make decisions—both thoughts and deeds—that are pleasing to God. I believe this type of power is often most evident during times of extreme challenge, during subtle encounters and in situations when it would be easier to follow Satan, society's dictates or our own (I examine these issues in detail later). So while it might *seem* as if a bearer of prejudice has power over a recipient (in this case, that Bob has power over Tom), from a Christian perspective, because Bob's prejudicial thought is ungodly, Bob actually has *diminished* power.

The concept of *peace* refers to an ability that enables Christians to reject disturbing, disquieting or upsetting thoughts or behavior that can result from negative experiences (Jn 14:27). It too is of divine origin and reflects the wherewithal to live in a state of relative spiritual calm even when we have had emotionally, physically and psychologically damaging experiences. Just as Christ exemplified spiritual power, the Bible includes many examples of his ability to respond in godly ways to negative situations. In my earlier example, as the recipient of prejudice, Tom may experience various negative consequences (for example, being avoided by Bob or being stereotyped) that diminish his resolve and result in internal conflict and negative feelings about himself as well as ungodly feelings and/or behavior toward Bob. It should be noted that peace does not suggest complacency or simply allowing negative things to occur, but rather reflects the ability to both work to combat prejudices and to have the intestinal fortitude to prevent them from overshadowing one's life. As Christians, God's peace can be elusive because of the problems and challenges we are often bombarded with on a daily basis, society's pressure to give an eye for an eye, and the human tendency toward self-protection. Yet an important element of peace that comes from God is its nature—it can be maintained in varied contexts, conditions and situations.

Both power and peace suggest intentionality on the part of persons involved—Bob's decision to think as he did as well as Tom's subsequent decision to respond in a certain way. A prejudicial encounter can be a challenge because persons are confronted with possible prejudices from varied sources. Furthermore, the topic of prejudices rarely reflects the simple scenario between Bob and Tom suggested here because it is possible to have prejudicial thoughts and beliefs and not act on them; it is also possible to behave in prejudicial ways (i.e., to discriminate) without having prejudicial thoughts and beliefs. (Note: scholarship suggests a strong link between prejudicial attitudes/beliefs and behavior, meaning that it is more common for persons who harbor prejudicial attitudes and beliefs to discriminate than for discrimination to occur without a prejudicial impetus.)

These two concepts—power and peace—will be examined in great detail. As a guiding premise in the book, I contend that those who are prejudiced limit God's power to work in and through them; those who experience prejudices may struggle with psychological and emotional turmoil that hinders them from receiving the full peace of God. The twofold effects of prejudices can also impact the same person, causing the recipient of prejudices to also become prejudiced. When this occurs, one must deal with both a lack of power *and* diminished peace. Either state is spiritually, emotionally and psychologically unhealthy. This book encourages the reader to strive for a more excellent life testimony for Christ and also provides information to inform others.

Each chapter of this book is divided into two sections to reflect the two parties that exist in a prejudicial situation. Information related to the *bearer* of prejudices (and gaining *power*) is presented in the first section of each chapter followed by information related to the *recipient* of prejudices (and gaining *peace*). Each section considers similar issues from a different perspective. Thus the first section of each chapter deals with overcoming prejudices for more spiritual power and ways in which prejudices can undermine God's power in our lives. Section two of each chapter links prejudices to diminished peace and addresses how recipients of prejudices can find God's peace.

As one who knows firsthand about such challenges, the principles presented in this book helped me achieve added spiritual peace as well as attain a more powerful Christian testimony. As an ordained minister, I undergird each section with Scripture and end each section with additional biblical passages to "read about" the topics of prejudices, power and peace in general. (Unless otherwise noted, Scripture references are based on the New Revised Standard Version of the Bible.) Because I am also a sociologist who studies various forms of *inequality, I have also incorporated material from sociology, sociology of religion and cultural studies research on the subject. In addition, from time to time, I include my own experiences and those of family members, friends and colleagues for illustrative purposes.[3] I also reference findings from an academic study I performed on the subject of prejudices, *racism and *racial reconciliation among a group of white and African American Christians. So this book is academic and applied as well as scholarly and spiritual in nature. The book's scope does not limit itself to racial or cultural issues but examines many types of prejudices. You as the reader are also asked to examine prejudices on a personal level such that God's power and peace can be attained on an individual basis. Only when each of us becomes aware and accountable and desires personal growth can we hope to see change on a larger scale. Scriptural references, research findings, practical applications, experiences and observations are included to illustrate how prejudices and their side effects can be identified and overcome. As Christians in search of spiritual power and peace, we continue to be challenged to identify and overcome personal shortcomings that hinder our service for God. It is my hope that, with this book as a tool, the Bible as the foundation, and the Holy Spirit as the inspirational guide, readers will be able to affect prejudice for power and peace as never before.

---

[3]Pseudonyms are used for names.

1

Awakenings and Beginnings

FOR POWER

In the beginning . . . God said, "Let us make humankind in our image, according to our likeness."

GENESIS 1:1, 26

Long before I was inspired to write this book, I traveled to Georgia to attend graduate school. A Christian for over twelve years, I had been born and raised in church. I cannot fully describe my excitement upon arriving in the "Bible Belt." I rented a car at the airport and immediately turned on the radio. The radio station was tuned to a church broadcast, which excited me all the more and seemed to confirm that my future experiences in Georgia would be positive, Spirit-filled ones. Needless to say, I was initially somewhat disillusioned to learn that my expectations had been naive and far too simplistic to fully explain the many facets of a Christian experience in a different locale. I had envisioned a spiritual Mecca, combined with the charm and style Southern living had to offer. Some experiences met and exceeded my expectations, while others fell short.

Some memories include isolation from male graduate-school peers; welcoming gestures at a class-diverse church; a study team with a *biracial male graduate student despite the objections of his friends; the friendly atmosphere at one job although I was the only African American in the department; a realtor's reluctance to show me a new home in an all white subdivision; tension between a singles ministry and some of the married women in a church; and the genuine and long-lasting friendship between myself and a white male coworker. These experiences, influenced by factors such as race, ethnicity, sex, class, gender, marital status and region, eventually spurred my academic and religious interests in the subjects of inequality, discrimination and gender/sex and race relations. In retrospect I have attempted to learn something from all of these experiences. Positive or negative, each has affected the type of person I am today. The positive experiences confirmed the continued good and intrinsic worth of humankind while the negative experiences reminded me of the reality of human frailty and enabled me to gain Christian character and exhibit the fruit of the Spirit (see Briscoe 1984). Please note that this book was not written to critique or praise a particular region, group or person, but to examine the issue of prejudice.

Exactly what is prejudice? Sociologists define prejudice as rigid, irrational, inaccurate beliefs or attitudes about others based largely on a faulty assessment of oneself and others. Prejudiced persons prejudge others and are inflexible in their views—even in the face of contradictory information or with little regard to facts. Although less known, prejudices can be negative or positive. Positive prejudice involves favorable, often exaggerated views about others (usually ourselves or people who are like us), for example, females believing that, in general, females are more sensitive and nurturing than males (although studies show that both sexes are just as capable of such emotions and behavior, but that females are more likely than males to be *taught* such things). Another example of positive prejudice germane to the classroom setting involves giving certain students the benefit of the doubt based on prejudices that suggest their inherent aptitude or abilities (e.g., a teacher gives an Asian student full credit for an incomplete or vaguely explained math exam response because he assumes Asians are good at math).[1] However, negative prejudices are more common and involve directly or indirectly devaluing and diminishing others. History and research show that people

[1]The reader should note that although these examples reflect positive prejudices for the recipients, nonrecipients are indirectly experiencing negative prejudices. In the math example, the grades of non-Asian students with incomplete or vague responses are negatively affected because they will not be given the benefit of the doubt on the exam.

often harbor negative prejudices.[2] Although prejudice is an attitude, it is common for prejudicial beliefs to lead to unequal treatment or behavior (also known as discrimination). As mentioned in the introduction, it is important to remember the distinction between prejudices (i.e., attitudes) and prejudice-related behavior or discrimination (i.e., behavior) and that, although they are often correlated, they are different.

In order to be prejudiced, a person must make some type of comparison between himself or herself and another person or group. After the relative comparison has been made, the prejudiced person comes to the conclusion that his "position" is superior. Let me explain by using a few well-known phrases: "I am better than you" infers that a comparison has been made and I (the prejudiced person) am somehow elevated or superior in status. References like "low-level" or "low-life" suggest that one is in some way high or higher than others. Studies show that it is common for people to hold prejudices based on factors such as race (i.e., *racism), ethnicity, nationality, religious preference, sex/gender (i.e., *sexism), age (i.e., *ageism), sexual orientation (i.e., *homophobia), foreign status (i.e., *xenophobia) or class (i.e., *classism). Prejudices may also exist based on less often considered factors such as skin color, body size, region, marital status, place of residence or educational level.[3]

Prejudice should not be confused with *preference*. These two words are often used interchangeably and incorrectly. *I prefer strawberry ice cream to chocolate ice cream* means that I like strawberry better, but I may like chocolate too. I prefer watching movies to sports. Preference is best associated with things or places and not people. If we prefer X people to Y people ("thin" people to "fat"; white to Asian; educated to less-educated; middle class to poor) we should ask ourselves why to make sure that we don't have subtle prejudices against the Y people. Preferences and prejudices both involve making choices. With prejudice, the wrong choice is made for the wrong reason.

Most people have had some experience involving prejudice; either

---

[2]Several academic works include Bobo 1988; Duckitt 1992; Feagin 1975; Gaertner and Dovidio 1986; Jackman 1977; Macionis 1999. An analysis from the Christian market is Tony Evans's (1995) *Let's Get to Know Each Other*.

[3]For additional foundational academic information on the subject, see both Merton's (1968) analysis of the basic dynamics of prejudices as well as Blumer's (1958) reader-friendly explanation of prejudice relative to group position.

we have had prejudicial thoughts or beliefs, we have discriminated, or we have been the recipient of prejudices and discrimination. These situations can make us, if not bitter, at least unsettled. Scripture challenges us to be in the world but not of the world. This means that although we live, work and function in society, our focus, motives and priorities are determined and driven by the desire to please God. Conflicts can be expected as we contend with Satan, pressure from the world and our own desires. However, when properly addressed, challenges can act as catalysts to draw us closer to God and strengthen our relationship with God.

One of the most important results of a strong relationship with God is power—the type of power that can change attitudes and behavior and transform lives (Schuller 1993). As noted in the introduction, I am not referring to control or authority in the earthly sense, but the capacity and fortitude to be intentional about exhibiting godly attitudes and behavior. One of the words most commonly translated as "power" in the Greek New Testament is *dunamis,* which means might, strength or miraculous power.[4] God's power can be thought of as a supernatural, eternal energy source. I would like to use a description based on the central concepts in this book. God can be thought of as the *Power Source,* Jesus as the *Power Line* and the Holy Spirit as our continual *Power Generator.* The Bible is our *Power Manual* to be used to identify the growth areas in our lives that require charges and recharges. When we accepted Jesus into our lives, we became forever plugged into the *Power Source.* Jesus is our connection to God—our mediator. The Holy Spirit provides us with comfort and direction, and the gospel is the "power of God for salvation" (Rom 1:16).

The Bible provides an illustration of power from God in Acts 1:8 that is germane to efforts to combat prejudices: "you will receive power when the Holy Spirit has come upon you; and you will be my witnesses in Jerusalem, in all Judea and Samaria, and to the ends of the earth." This Scripture informs us about what we have, what we are to do with it and where we are to do it. Notice a few things about this passage. The phrase "will receive" shows us that, when we become Christians, our receipt of power from God is a given. Also notice that the Holy Spirit (our *Power*

[4]The word *dynamic* in the English language is a derivative of *dunamis.*

Generator) has to be involved in order to see results. What should we do with this power? We are to be witnesses, of course. Where? Looking at a map of the Holy Land, Jerusalem is located west of the Dead Sea, Judea is just north of Jerusalem, and Samaria is quite a distance north of Judea. Is Jesus instructing us to go to these places? Probably not. He is saying, "go." He wants us to be witnesses for him near and far. The phrase "to the ends of the earth" means wherever we go—and to whomever we meet. Central to witnessing is our lifestyle—our attitudes, beliefs and behavior on a day-to-day basis. The power of God gives Christians many abilities (and responsibilities) not shared by non-Christians. Divine power gives us the ability to meet the challenges of the Great Commission in Matthew 28:19. We view life differently and thus act and react differently when faced with difficult situations, societal pressures or the desire to follow our own dictates. This divine power also enables us to handle potentially negative experiences positively.[5]

In addition to references to power in the Bible, research has also examined power struggles. If you have taken a course in sociology, political science or even cultural studies, you've probably been introduced to conflict theory (Marx [1848] 1977). Although the theory was originally developed to explain inequality and power struggles in industrialized Europe, its tenets have been found to be broadly applicable across many societies. Simply put, according to this theory, persons in power in society (those in control of major economic resources) attempt to maintain their positions of power while those without power attempt to acquire power. Such societies are fraught with problems due to inherent inequality because a few are powerful, wealthy and prosperous at the expense of the many who are less so. An important facet of this theory suggests that arenas and institutions in society such as politics, religion, the military, the media and belief systems often perpetuate group power struggles and social problems. Based on this premise, prejudices are one way that inequality can be perpetuated and justified. This theory applies here because it helps to explain the societal context for some negative attitudes and behavior among groups and individuals. It can also be used

---

[5]Tony Evans (1995) *Let's Get to Know Each Other;* Raleigh Washington and Glen Kehrein (1996) *Breaking Down Walls: A Model for Reconciliation in An Age of Racial Strife;* Spencer Perkins and Chris Rice (2000) *More Than Equals;* Gerald Sittser (1994) *Loving Across Our Differences.*

to show how earthly power struggles negatively affect some people in tangible ways and can stand in opposition to Christian tenets—but can be counteracted using divine power.

An example of how prejudices can be somewhat subtle but have far reaching effects and reflect power dynamics, can be seen in prejudice based on age and educational attainment. College professors, by virtue of the lengthy and rigorous process required to obtain their credentials, are generally older and have more formal education than their students and most persons in the larger society. One of my Christian colleagues is very good at placing these attributes in the proper perspective. Dr. James teaches undergraduate statistics. As you might imagine, many students find this course unnerving; the class requires mastery of statistical theory and techniques, extensive writing and application of material learned in other undergraduate classes. To make matters worse, the class is one of two required courses for graduation. Having taught statistics, I know what a challenge this can be. This type of class can be stressful for both professors and students.

It is common for some professors to downplay (or in some cases ignore) comments by students about the difficulty of their classes. We've taken such classes in the past (and usually more advanced classes as well), determined the syllabus and assignments and basically know the answers to the various course assignments, exams and projects. Thus our educational status and related skills may make it difficult to relate to students who are struggling. It is also easy for professors to believe that student complaints are exaggerated and that students could master the material if they spent more time studying and less time goofing off and partying. Dr. James does not take this approach to teaching. Although she is aware that some students wish to earn good grades with minimal effort or attempt to manipulate her to improve their grades, Dr. James goes to great lengths to minimize power inequities based on possible ageism, educational level and sometimes elitism that can manifest themselves in the college classroom. Although she has more education and is older than her students, Dr. James tries to consider students the way she considers herself. For example, she provides midterm class evaluations to actively get student input at the midpoint of each semester. These evaluations enable her to identify strengths as well as drawbacks in the class, suggested strategies from students and, most importantly, ways to intervene to assist students *before* the end of the semester (when it is too late to master the material or improve a grade). Although students must complete the same material, they have other options in the class to help bolster grades, garner class participation points and help develop self-evaluation criteria. Dr. James has also revised facets of her class based on patterns of suggestions from students. Because of her hands-on teaching style, openness to students and continued efforts to improve her teaching methods, Dr. James has earned numerous teaching awards.

I applaud her ability to really *listen* to students, trust that they have valuable comments and suggestions to make, and realize that although she has skills and experiences that most of them have yet to acquire, they too have something to offer to strengthen the classroom learning experience. I also believe that in addition to statistics, by her example, Dr. James helps students to understand the importance of mutual respect, trust, openness and teamwork. As the "expert" based on education and age (older people are often assumed to be wiser and more trustworthy than younger persons), she could easily dismiss student concerns and simply exert her *power* in the class as the professor. Although she does not alter her class format based on the whims of students, Dr. James provides an excellent example of the type of *discernment that is needed to temper societal power differences and use *divine power* to teach in ways that can benefit students professionally and personally.

I'm sure most of us can recall a particularly trying situation when we could have said or done something that we would have later regretted. Instead, to the surprise of those involved (and maybe even to ourselves), we handled the challenge in a way that was pleasing to God. In retrospect, I'm sure you would agree that God's influence (i.e., God's power) caused this behavior. Our actions (what we say, but most importantly how we live from day to day) enable others to see Christ in us. This, in turn, may convict them to want to learn about the Jesus who caused such a change in our lives. We are also able to see results (fruit) of our actions (labor). Although God's power is available when we accept Jesus Christ, most of us tap into it at different times and in different ways. The desire for earthly power may divert our attention from heavenly things and some types of power are physically harmful (like electrical shock), but we can't have too much of God's power.

Many of us never fully avail ourselves of the heavenly power that is within our grasp because we allow people, situations, attitudes and behavior to distract us. Prejudice is one such distraction. Some readers might be thinking, *Surely prejudices don't exist among* true *Christians. People who have prejudices are obviously not saved but are hypocrites!* Satan (and the world) would like us to believe that our imperfect thoughts and actions mean that we are not *really* saved and cannot be useful to God. He wants us to believe this so that we will waste valuable time second-guessing our salvation, browbeating ourselves and feeling guilty, instead of striving to improve our Christian character by overcoming personal shortcomings.

We are challenged to ask the question, *Do I harbor prejudices toward others?* For example, do I think I am better than or superior to this or that person or group of people based on factors such as ethnicity, race, sex or class? Do I discriminate? Have I ever treated someone poorly because of these types of factors? Have I ever *refrained* from treating someone in a positive way because of such factors? These questions seem simple initially, but to determine honest responses may involve a complicated process of personal soul-searching, fasting, reading, listening and prayer. Speaking openly and honestly will help us to identify areas that need growth, determine why we feel and behave as we do and, through the direction of the Holy Spirit, find solutions to rid us of prejudices. For a Christian who has met the challenge and overcome prejudices, remembering how she or he overcame can be a valuable testimony for those who are about to attempt this challenge. He or she can provide an example of the truth that God can and will change lives if we desire to grow spiritually and are willing to work at it. Many people may not be aware that a certain statement, action or phrase is considered prejudicial. We may unknowingly offend others out of lack of awareness. If a person is unaware of a bias, he or she is incapable of changing—not even aware of the need for change (Gaertner and Dovidio 1986). This is where the discerning Christian can be most helpful, gently guiding the person to uncover his or her bias (Washington and Kehrein 1996; Perkins and Rice 2000).

Although some persons refer to the concepts interchangeably, sociologists generally distinguish between sex (female, male) and gender (woman, man). Although both are *socially constructed, the former term tends to be used when referring to biological differences between the two groups (e.g., hormonal differences, body size, reproductive processes), while the latter term is usually related to culturally based descriptions and differences in attitudinal and behavioral expectations between the groups (for example, traditional gender characterizations suggest that men are aggressive and women are submissive or men are "hard" and women are "soft"). In this book, when a topic is related to both concepts, I use the terminology *sex/gender* to remind readers of the distinction and linkage between the two concepts. The following example focuses on the issue of sex/gender to illustrate the possible subtle manifestations of some prejudices.

I was once employed at a consulting firm that could be described as integrated based on the sex make-up of its employees. An almost equal number of males and females held management and nonmanagement positions. *Diversity existed from top management throughout the entire company to the extent that the president was female and the company employed male administrative assistants. During a project it was often necessary to meet with clients at their places of business. Connie, a female assistant vice president, once spoke of an experience she had with a certain client. The client's company could be described as a traditional organization in that the majority of the persons employed in middle and upper management positions were male. The firm did employ females, but mainly as staff persons and secretaries. Connie was a very knowledgeable member of our consulting firm with many years of experience. The client was an older male with years of tenure at his company. His many years in the business industry spoke well of his leadership skills and wisdom in making sound business decisions.

The client regarded the client-vendor relationship as vital and was spending a great deal of money and time to acquire our products and services. Connie noted that although she enjoyed working with this client, one tendency—calling her "girl"—upset her. During meetings and telephone conversations, he continually used the term *girl* when addressing her. It seemed as if he often used *girl* as a substitute for Connie's name!

Although she promptly (and frequently) corrected him, this continued throughout the course of the project. This client may not have realized that his use of this word upset Connie. It would seem as if her frequent corrections would have triggered the correct response from him when addressing her. However, this was not the case. It seemed extremely difficult for him to change his behavior. Initially he may not have been aware that the term *girl* could be perceived negatively. He may have associated sexist terms with vulgar, lewd language and not realized that although the word *girl* was an acceptable way to describe young females, it was not appropriate when addressing an adult woman and business colleague.

Historically, because of *systemic forces associated with sexism (sex-based prejudicial attitudes and/or behavior) and in some cases, personal choices, women have been less likely to hold or expect to hold positions of power and influence in society (Bonilla-Santiago 1992; McRae 1986; Ortiz 1991; Pearce 1983). Although great strides have been made, many women continue to experience tangible and more covert forms of inequality linked to various forms of sex-based prejudice. For example, research suggests that (1) female-headed households have increased; (2) unmarried women with children are more likely to bear the brunt of economic and noneconomic support for their children; and (3) women tend to earn 70 to 77 cents to every dollar earned by men. These factors have all contributed to increased *poverty among women (Brown 1997; Eggebeen and Lichter 1991; Ortiz 1991; Tienda, Donato and Cordero-Guzman 1992. See also King 1992). Although Connie's experience may pale in comparison to more life-changing economic, political, emotional and psychological challenges often associated with sexism, her situation is indicative of the larger social reality.

There is no easy way to put it: harboring prejudices reflects ungodliness. It can be thought of as a large stone tied around our necks. It is extremely heavy and prevents spiritual movement. Initially it will only slightly slow us down, but the more we walk, the heavier the weight gets, until we are no longer able to make progress. Prejudices can prevent Christians from moving freely for the Lord and can eventually weigh us down to the point that we have difficulty living as God would like (Sittser 1994; Ford 1994). But spiritual and practical benefits come from proactively striving to move beyond barriers such as prejudices.

During the first few years at a previous job I was the only African American in my department. The position required quite a bit of travel and meetings with many types of people. As such, I would often find myself traveling with coworkers to a client's place of business. As time progressed, it became obvious to me that although most of my coworkers were friendly, good-natured people and very professional to work with, they had not and did not interact with many African Americans. This was surprising to me but has been confirmed in many studies on the infrequency of sustained interaction across racial and ethnic lines (Massey and Denton 1993; Wilson 1996). In the past I too had been guilty of working with non-African Americans without usually becoming close friends. However, during this employment phase, I found myself becoming friends with coworkers. We had in-depth discussions, comparing and contrasting our histories, backgrounds and cultures. We even discussed things as inconsequential as hair care. On occasions, we would find ourselves saying, "I didn't know that" or "Isn't that fascinating" regarding our differences. We also discovered that we were more alike than we thought (Evans 1995). These instances were not racially heated in the least, merely learning experiences where all persons involved departed the better for having talked. These experiences helped me (and my coworkers also, I would warrant) better understand that being different is not better or worse, just different.

READ ABOUT

- **The Power Available Through the Holy Spirit:** Acts 10
- **How to Obtain Power:** Acts 1

FOR PEACE

Indeed, the word of God is living and active, sharper than any two-edged sword, piercing until it divides soul from spirit, joints from marrow; it is able to judge the thoughts and intentions of the heart.

HEBREWS 4:12

Typically, we assume that bearers of prejudice are a different group from victims of prejudice. This is often the case. But not only is prejudice generally negative, it can also affect the same person in different ways. It is important to remember that the same person can experience prejudice and *also* harbor prejudice. What types of experiences do victims of prejudice face? In what ways are they affected by prejudice? How can prejudice be linked to a lack of godly peace? Can solutions be found such that persons who experience prejudice can tap in to the peace that is only available from God? Where should they begin this journey toward peace? Prejudices based on race and ethnicity are common offenders against peace.

Race and *ethnicity* are related terms, but with slightly different meanings. Sociologists suggest that both concepts, like sex/gender, are socially constructed, that is, created in society, based on culture and vary across societies and groups. Race has generally and broadly been defined as a category of people that have biologically transmitted traits in common (e.g., skin color, hair texture, facial features). Historically, biologists used such traits to categorize persons for *descriptive* reasons—Caucasoid (today's whites), Negroid (blacks) and Mongoloid (Asians) was the basic typology. Over time, these descriptions became codified such that group differences for outcomes such as aptitude and economic progress were suggested based on claims of biological validity that tend to ignore or downplay factors such as unequal opportunity, unequal access and discrimination. And although there is no "pure" racial group, society often categorizes and ranks persons based on race and attributes varying amounts of social status to one's racial designation. Poor race relations have resulted, in part, because groups have ascribed judgments, moral evaluations, stereotypes and disparaging characteristics to racial designations (Omi and Winant 1994; Roediger 1994; West 1993).

Ethnicity is usually associated with connections to countries and lands and refers to descriptions such as Italian American (persons of Italian and American descent) or African American (persons of African and American descent). Both terms (race and ethnicity) have been shown to reflect varying customs and lifestyles. Some persons use the terms interchangeably (i.e., blacks or African Americans). However, the recent United States census provided options to identify one's race and ethnicity, suggesting a move toward continued distinctions between the two concepts (Nagel 1994).

Furthermore, racial or ethnic prejudice and prejudice based on skin color are related, but can also manifest themselves differently. Racial and ethnic groups have been identified based on different skin colors (or at least we think we can identify them). For example, blacks tend to have darker skin than whites, and Puerto Ricans may be darker toned than some Cubans. For those who harbor prejudice based on race or ethnicity, these visual cues provide them with the "information" needed to think or behave poorly toward such persons (Gallagher 1999; Kirschenman and Neckerman 1991; Waters 1999). It is also important to consider *intragroup discrimination based on skin color where, say, some lighter-skinned minorities may harbor ill feelings against their darker-skinned counterparts and vice versa (Russell, Wilson and Hall 1992).

Although there is a large body of academic literature on race relations and racism, some researchers fail to consider the emotional and psychological effects of race-based prejudice. I believe this omission is partly due to the nature of some academic research, which can be distant and unattached, and also due to the often greater difficulty of investigating the many nuances of emotions and feelings. However, scholars and mainstream writers are attempting to tackle this subject. For example, in *Race Matters* (1993) Cornel West provides academic and social commentary on contemporary race relations in the United States. The author examines the role of race in shaping the experiences of many African Americans,[6] especially poor and disenfranchised inner-city residents. Although West illustrates how "race" continues to "matter" economically and politically, his description of the emotional and psychological toll of racism is important to consider. According to West, historic and current racism hurts recipients emotionally and psychologically. He points to a growing nihilism and angst among some urban African Americans reflected in lovelessness, hopelessness and meaninglessness that affect how persons view themselves, view others and interact in society. For the author, continued poor race relations stymie all involved and prevent us from recognizing our common Americanness and humanness. (For research on the debilitating effects of poor race relations on our country,

---

[6]The reader should note that although West's title, *Race Matters,* suggests that the term "black" is more appropriate here, I tend to use "African American" in the book.

also refer to Omi and Winant 1994; Roediger 1991; and Jaret 1995.) Applying West's observations to this book, persons who experience "isms" (e.g., classism, sexism, racism, ageism) may lack inner peace and have difficulty living peacefully with others. Other scholars have also been successful at performing academic studies *and* presenting some of the everyday implications of their results (see West 1993; Billingsley 1992; Blumer 1958; Omi and Winant 1994; Roediger 1991)—but some of us know about these everyday implications firsthand.

My first memory of differences in skin color occurred when I was about five years old. Up until that time, my family had lived in an all African American neighborhood and most of my friends and playmates were African American children. As far as I can remember, most of my teachers were also African American. Then my family moved to a racially mixed neighborhood. I did not know about racism or discrimination or even understand the terms *race* or *ethnicity;* I only knew that our neighbors were a different color. The topics of race and racial differences never came up in my home, and since my parents were devout Christians, we were raised to love and appreciate others.

Because we were all about the same age, my sisters and I often played with the neighbor's children. Our families were also very similar; our parents were in the same age group, our houses were about the same size, and we were in a similar economic bracket. I don't know to what religious faith our neighbors belonged, but I can remember them leaving for church service on Sunday mornings. The experience I'm referring to occurred one day when we were out playing in our backyard with the neighbor's kids. I don't remember all the details, only that the neighbor's children called my sisters and me the proverbial N word. I did not really understand the word: I only knew by their tone that it was not a very nice thing to call someone. Since up until that point we had all been friends, I began to struggle with a multitude of emotions: positive memories of happiness and joy based on the many fun times we had shared and negative feelings of hurt, anger and betrayal regarding what had recently happened. To some degree I refused to fully believe what had happened because if I did, I thought that it would forever change the way I viewed my friends. My little mind was in complete turmoil; I had never experienced such mental trauma before.

The saying "children can be cruel" was never so appropriate as in this instance. My hurt feelings were not due totally to what was said, but also *how* it was said. In retrospect, their tone seemed very belittling and degrading, as if we were somehow subhuman. I tried to rationalize the reasons behind their meanness. My thoughts ranged from *Was it something we did or said to deserve such treatment?* to *What would happen tomorrow?* I also wondered, *Could we ever be "real" friends again?* and *Did I want to be?* One incident had changed the relationship, not only between us children, but between our parents as well. We asked my mother why the neighbor's children had called us names.

My mother, attempting to be diplomatic, tried to explain as best she could. She stated that, when people are angry, they may say things they don't really mean. She also said that some people thought they were better than others and might try to convey that message through words and actions. As I've gotten older and better understand these two methods for instilling prejudices, I've learned to confront and combat prejudices, sometimes prayerfully overlooking the former and being cautious of the latter, other times acting to address them both. And although the latter approach of conveying negative messages through actions presents a more immediate danger, the force and effect of *words* should not be underestimated. Here is a somewhat different example of how words (or the lack of them) can be damaging.

I often teach controversial and emotionally sensitive classes and topics related to racism, sexism and classism. Most of my classes consist of white students from somewhat rural areas and minority students who are experiencing isolation on a predominately white campus. And most of the students have had limited exposure to the course subjects. As you might expect, many students would rather avoid discussing these subjects and have spent a great deal of their lives ignoring issues of race, class and gender—for various reasons. Peter was a somewhat quiet white male in my class on the African American family. In addition to exams and papers, students were also graded on class participation. Although he was earning decent grades (he had a high C average in the class), Peter rarely made comments during class discussions. I noticed that Peter had few class participation points. When I opened the floor for student comments, he was silent. If I asked him a question directly,

Peter would try to mumble something, but it was usually incoherent and strained. As the semester proceeded, I met with Peter to discuss his progress. I told him candidly that because of his low class participation grade, he would probably earn a C or lower in the class. I asked him why he seemed uncomfortable speaking in class.

After a long pause, Peter admitted that although he understood the readings and was making progress in the class, he was reluctant to speak up in class because he didn't know exactly *what to say*. He wanted to make comments about the African American family, but he was afraid of using the wrong words. He did not want to offend me or African American students in the class or appear to be racist. He admitted that he had been raised in a household where some members of his family made subtle but negative comments about minorities and that as a result of my class he realized that they harbored prejudices. He was concerned that because he had not been able to even recognize prejudices among his own family members, he might naively make a comment in class that was actually a prejudicial statement and not even know it! Peter was clearly distraught. And he had been afraid to speak to me about the situation for fear that I might not believe him. I did believe Peter. He had been afraid of using the *wrong words* in class and thus had decided not to use *any words* at all. I encouraged Peter to make comments in class and not to be afraid of being honest. I also explained to him that, as the professor, it was my responsibility to help him in this area, such that he could learn and grow. I remember Peter's experience each time I teach a controversial or sensitive subject and work intentionally to create a teaching/learning space that fosters honest communication and dialogue.

Words are the primary way in which we communicate, interact with others and express ourselves. In many cases, our ability to master the human language and effectively use it can profoundly affect the masses (Gandhi and Martin Luther King Jr. made powerful use of language) (Morris 1984). In contrast, Peter's experience illustrates how the absence of words can be stifling and painful. I also thought about my awakening childhood experience and how that one word had affected all the people involved. I thought, if one word could do damage, cause hurt feelings, disassociation and mistrust, surely there were other words that could have the opposite effect. Profound words can be found in many books and literature, but none as thought-provoking and convicting as the Word of God. Through the ages, its ability to change hearts, shape lives and alter behavior has been surpassed by no other book. Since this is the case, I wondered what the Word of God has to say about prejudice and finding peace. Has God given us Scripture that we can practically apply to our everyday lives? The answer, of course, is *yes!*

God's Word gives us guidelines for peace. But first we must revisit the question, "Exactly what is peace?" Consider the following tropical scene. Imagine that you are floating along in cool, tranquil waters. Silence envelopes you except for the slow murmur of the waves as they meet the shore. In the far distance, you can hear the faint call of exotic birds. A cool breeze is present but unneeded due to the temperate climate. The sun provides inviting warmth and a perfect complement to the setting. Within your grasp are the necessities of life—food, water and shelter—but no people can be found for miles. This type of scene is often associated with peace. In fact, many people choose isolated, remote vacation spots specifically because these places represent peaceful, restful havens. Sometimes at work, I have found myself anticipating such a getaway, especially on a particularly trying day (in fact, the majority of my vacations have been to such places).

Before we go further, let's determine some additional working definitions for peace. A Greek word for peace, *hēsuchia,* means stillness, quietness, silence or without bustle. Peace can thus be defined as a state of quiet or tranquility. Several other definitions include, "the tranquility of order,"[7] "freedom from disquieting or oppressive thoughts or emotions" or "harmony in personal relationships."[8] All of these definitions can be used as we think about how recipients of prejudice can find peace. Although my example of the peaceful vacation spot seems wonderful, we cannot, of course, find peace in a person, place or thing. Any attempt to do so may bring temporary results but eventual disappointment. Let's establish one truth at the outset: true peace is only possible as a result of a relationship with God through Jesus Christ. As noted in the introductory chapter, the type of peace to which I am referring is not shaped or

---

[7]Definition by Augustine of Hippo as taken from Briscoe (1994).

[8]For additional insight and definitions of peace, refer to H. Bloomfield's (1996) *Making Peace with Yourself* and Briscoe's (1984) *The Fruit of the Spirit.*

influenced by one's situation or context, but is divine in nature and enables persons to combat negative situations and experiences such as prejudices. Given that, some readers might think, *Well enough said. Why do I need to continue to read this book?* Well, continue to read so that we can address the following questions:

- What is God's definition of peace as provided in Scripture?
- How is God's definition similar or different from human definitions?
- How can prejudice affect a person's peace?
- How can a person who has experienced prejudice gain the peace of God?
- Why is God's peace necessary for our Christian testimony and ministry?

Peace is mentioned many times in the Bible. In order to get a better understanding of the concept, let's look at various Scriptures that help to define peace. I am always cautious about "Bible hopping" (jumping from verse to verse in various chapters based on the inclusion of a certain word without considering possible differences in context and application),[9] but each of these references provides important points about peace.

> Peace I leave with you; my peace I give to you. I do not give to you as the world gives. Do not let your hearts be troubled, and do not let them be afraid. (Jn 14:27)

In this passage Jesus was speaking with his disciples about the coming of the Holy Spirit and granting them peace. This Scripture is full of words to remember. First notice that Jesus *left* peace with us. This means that peace is available to us here and now. Also notice that Jesus gave peace to us, so it's not necessary to go places, do things or search out people to attain it. The next phrase is key: the peace that Jesus gives us is *totally different* from the peace offered by the world. So although the secular definitions of peace may seem similar to biblical definitions, they are not the same because the *source* of peace differs. This Scripture also associ-

---

[9]Biblical scholars are cautioned against proof-texting so that Scripture is not taken out of context (G. Wilmore 1994, 1995). However, there are universal themes in Scripture (e.g., the call to love everyone unconditionally, God's role throughout history, the challenge to forsake sin). I contend that peace, as evidence of Christian character, is one such universal (Gal 5:16-26).

ates Christ's peace with "an untroubled heart" and "a fearless heart."

> And the peace of God, which surpasses all understanding, will guard your hearts and your minds in Christ Jesus. (Phil 4:7)

This Scripture informs us that true peace originates with God. This type of peace cannot be comprehended because it surpasses what is earthly imaginable—it is heavenly. God's peace will preserve both our hearts and minds.

> For he is our peace; in his flesh he has made both groups into one and has broken down the dividing wall, that is, the hostility between us. (Eph 2:14)

> And let the peace of Christ rule in your hearts, to which indeed you were called in the one body. And be thankful. (Col 3:15)

Both Scriptures have similar references to peace. Both passages tell of unity. Jesus Christ is presented as the one that brings divided people together. This is very important to mention within the context of this book because prejudices usually divide those involved.

> Now may the Lord of peace himself give you peace at all times in all ways. The Lord be with all of you. (2 Thess 3:16)

At the conclusion of Paul's second letter to the believers in Thessalonica, he gave the above words of encouragement. Again, the Lord is described as the source of peace. Also notice that according to Paul the Lord's peace is available all the time and in all ways. Just looking at these passages gives us insight into some scriptural definitions for peace and the many areas of our lives that it can affect. Let's recap our findings. God's peace is

- evidence of Christian character
- everlasting
- different from the world's peace
- able to sustain our hearts and minds
- able to keep our hearts trouble free and fearless
- available even when we don't know how and why
- able to bind together divided people

And like God's power, the more peace we have the better!

Peace is one of the fruits of the Spirit (Gal 5:16-26) with both spiritual and practical implications. When we exhibit this fruit, it gives evidence of our relationship with God, others and self. In *Fruit of the Spirit,* Stuart Briscoe (1984) suggests that Christians who have peace have (1) peace with God, reflecting total submission to God and awareness that God is in control of our lives; (2) peace with others, reflected in the ability to interact and live harmoniously with others—even those who do not reciprocate; and (3) the peace of God, which reflects inner peace of the mind and heart. According to Briscoe, although the world defines peace as the absence of adversity and negativity, as Christians, we define peace as the presence of God. Therefore, godly peace suggests that, because of a relationship with God through Jesus Christ, one can counteract prejudice (i.e., others with limited or no godly power) and its potential damaging effects on self-esteem, self-confidence and the ability to exhibit the other dimensions of the fruit of the Spirit. One who exhibits godly peace is also in a position of power!

Earlier I noted the roles that God, Jesus Christ and the Holy Spirit play in our gaining spiritual power. Well, the Trinity plays a similar role in finding peace. Using the second central concept from this book—peace—God can be thought of as the *Source of Peace,* Jesus as the *Peace Maker* and the Holy Spirit as the *Peace Generator.* Heavenly, everlasting peace is only available from God, through Jesus Christ, with the help of the Holy Spirit. In their book *More Than Equals: Racial Healing for the Sake of the Gospel* Spencer Perkins and Chris Rice (2000) provide testimony and evidence of God's power to bring about peaceful, harmonious relationships. With God's guidance and lots of plain old hard work, Perkins and Rice were able to transcend society's race-related traps and forge a lasting friendship as "yokefellows"—Christians who had to believe and behave as equals in order to forward God's ministry. Interestingly, many of their obstacles were not due to problems between the two men, but rather were a result of strife and misunderstandings around them. However, despite external stresses, Perkins and Rice chose to have peace as individuals and in their relationship.

Similarly, academic findings from Omi and Winant's (1994) study can also be applied to our understanding of obstacles to peace in general.

In *Racial Formation in the United States from the 1960s to the 1990s,* the authors present a theory of racial formation and analyze key historical events. They contend that the U.S. economic, social, cultural and particularly the political arenas have been shaped by "racial projects"—the tendency to purposely use race (fears about racial differences and losing power to other racial groups) to divide groups along racial lines. These racial projects pit groups with possible commonalities against each other and result in reduced empathy for others and the failure to work to address social injustices. They present examples of the prominence given to race in our society and the ways in which race has been and continues to be redefined by various political interest groups. Using their terminology, I contend that peace can be undermined, not only by racial projects, but also by "class projects," "sex projects," "age projects," "nationality projects"—any concerted effort to use group distinctions to divide and conquer and engender unrest. An example of classism experienced by one of my students supports my assertion.

While completing graduate school I was employed at a school for "underachievers." Middle and high school students who had fallen behind at other schools attended this school to get back on track; some attended the school for several semesters and then reentered their previous school, while others would graduate from this expensive, private academy. A large percentage of students attended this academy because of behavioral problems at their previous institutions. Thus the school became somewhat of a last resort for wayward kids from privileged families—and students who attended the academy were somewhat stigmatized in the exclusive circles in which their families traveled. However, a few of the students were not from wealthy families; Thomas was one such student. Thomas had been part of a pretty wealthy family, but after his parents were divorced, he was being raised alone by his mother. His father, although wealthy, was absent and inconsistent with child support payments. Thomas had been a disciplinary problem at several previous public high schools, and his mother was working several jobs to pay for his tuition at the academy. She believed that only this level of intervention could save her son from a life of drugs and mayhem.

Thomas's involvement at the academy had provided some of the structure, discipline and support he needed. His grades improved in the smaller-sized classes and he made fewer disruptions. He also became somewhat close to several of the female teachers, myself included. Although Thomas was doing better in school, he was having some difficulty establishing friends. Because he was not part of a wealthy family, Thomas felt inadequate as compared to his classmates. They drove expensive luxury or sports cars to school or were driven to school by chauffeurs and nannies; his mother dropped him off on her way to work in an old Buick. Although students wore uniforms to school (preventing visible class distinctions based on attire), Thomas knew that his lifestyle was very different from his peers. To make matters worse, he was ostracized by certain groups of wealthy students and not invited to their weekend activities and parties. Thomas was not in their "class" and they let him know it. Thomas felt dejected, devalued and inferior to his classmates. He complained about his economic status (Why didn't he have a BMW like his classmates?) and his life (Why did he have to attend a school for *losers?*). He also blamed his mother for his family's *fall* from economic and social grace (It's her fault we are poor. Why couldn't she stay married?). Thomas had little peace in his life.

Thus, students who as a group had experienced stigma associated with attending a school for underachievers (I often wondered who chose such a problematic name for the academy), chose to take part in a "class project" (applying Omi and Winant's terms) to divide each other along economic lines. They decided which students were worthy of group admission based on family wealth and social standing and intentionally excluded the others and labeled them as unworthy. Although several of us teachers attempted to encourage Thomas and remind him of his worth and potential, it seemed easier for him to believe the disparaging comments and actions of his peers than our words of encouragement. (I believe our status as both teachers *and* adults made this difficult as well—Thomas felt that we were too far removed from his situation to be able to relate.) As Thomas's lack of peace grew, he again became disruptive in class and was eventually expelled from the academy.

Despite the many obstacles to peace found in society, the Bible provides many references on the subject. Let's look at the example from the time Jesus took a boat to the other side of the sea in Mark 4:37-41. Jesus had just taught the people using parables and was on his way to the country of the Gadarenes. While he was on the boat, a fierce storm arose. Great winds blew and waves beat upon the vessel. Jesus, who was asleep in the back of the boat, was awakened by the fearful men. Everyone on board (except Jesus, of course) was afraid that the boat would be destroyed. What did Jesus do? He got up and rebuked the wind. Yes, he commanded the winds to stop blowing. He then commanded the sea to stop raging by uttering three words, "Peace! Be still." The Bible describes the result as "a dead calm."

Since Jesus said the word "peace" and "a dead calm" came over the storm, we will add this to our biblical definition of peace. What took place aboard that boat can be compared to many experiences in our lives. Dealing with prejudices can cause mental and emotional storms in our lives. We feel as if life is tossing us to and fro. On the one hand we must deal with *this* prejudice (the wind) and on the other hand we are confronted with *that* prejudice (the waves). Like those in that boat in the biblical story, we feel totally out of control—in some cases it may seem as if we are destined for destruction. During these rough times, try to recall how the people on the boat reacted. According to Scripture, they didn't waste time lowering life rafts or trying to weigh anchor. No, they went straight to the one they knew could solve the problem—they went straight to Jesus! The same way that Christ calmed the winds and seas aboard that boat, he can do so in our lives.

People, places and things cannot bring us peace. However, God can act through many people, places and things to help us attain peace. As Christians, we are encouraged to strive to attain personal peace and help others to do so. History is full of examples of periods of upheaval and unrest based on group conflict: World War I, race riots in Watts, the Vietnam War, forced internment of Japanese Americans after Pearl Harbor, César Chávez's fight for the rights of Hispanic workers, and more recently, the September 11 terrorist attacks.[10] And afterwards it required (and continues to require) years to repair the physical damage. And it

---

[10]Although there are a myriad of references to list, the reader should note the following books on historic conflict and unrest: Shapiro and Sullivan (1964) *Race Riots;* Mitchell (1970) *Race Riots in Black and White;* Conroy and Wray, eds. (1964) *Pearl Harbor Reexamined;* H. Barnes (1972) *Pearl Harbor After a Quarter of a Century;* Griswold del Castillo and Garcia (1995) *César Chávez: A Triumph of Spirit;* and Hall (1947) *World Wars and Revolutions: The Course of Europe Since 1900.*

typically took even longer to rebuild trust and relationships and restore peace. Although these events evidence the devastating effects of an absence of peace at a societal level, they also inform us about the potential damage individuals experience when they lack peace.

As this book unfolds, readers will be challenged to examine and consider the spiritual and practical implications of how a relationship with the Trinity, instruction from the Bible, understanding of the possible influences of Satan, the world and a focus on self—and the ability to choose—are all related to addressing prejudices. However, the goal is much more than mere academic or theological discussion and analysis, but a call to action. For example, we should not stop with considering the influence of the Holy Spirit in arresting prejudicial thoughts and behavior. Likewise, acknowledging God's infinite power to alter lives is only part of the process. Responding to prejudices for power and peace does require prayer, patience and reliance on God. It also requires Christians to act and serve as *change agents in the world. Doing so will require *both* spiritual wherewithal and human *agency.

READ ABOUT

- **Christ and Peace:** Isaiah 9:6
- **Holiness, Blamelessness and Peace:** Psalm 37:37-38; Hebrews 12:14-15
- **Christian Influence and Peace:** Mark 9:50
- **Peace and the Fruit of the Spirit:** Galatians 5:22-23

2

We Are All God's Creation

FOR POWER

Whoever does the will of God is my brother and sister and mother.

MARK 3:35

Many of us associate with different groups of people on a day-to-day basis, but we tend to migrate toward or interact most closely with those whose interests, ideas, background and beliefs are similar to ours. In sociological circles, this tendency is referred to as *homogamy (McCormick and Jesser 1988; Macionis 1999). Unlike the saying, "opposites attract," people tend to be drawn toward those with whom they have something in common. Well, what does a Christian secretary have in common with a Christian writer or with a Christian CEO? Of course, they are all Christians. No matter where we go, if we meet a Christian, we should feel an immediate commonality, an ever-present bond; we both know Christ. There is always something to talk about. Try swapping stories about life-changing events and blessings. The message of salvation is universal for Christians, no mater how diverse. So the next time you meet a Christian with whom you feel uneasy, remind yourself, "He's like me. We are both Christians." In doing so, the similarities found in a common religious and spiritual history can overshadow differences.

Let's look at the prayer in Matthew 6:9-13. It begins, "our Father."[1] Note the possessive term "our" and the noun "Father." Since the Lord is the par-

[1]Although I attempt to use gender inclusive terminology throughout this book, Matthew 6:9-13 is examined here as biblically written.

ent of us all, this makes us brothers and sisters. Some Christians greet each other at church with "brother" and "sister," but many of us have never really thought about the spiritual implications of these titles—and that the same words apply to *all* Christians. A common spiritual "bloodline" links us to God *and* to each other. That bloodline is in the person of Jesus Christ. Through "spiritual genetics" (if you will), all Christians are related (notice how our commonalities are increasing). What about Christians and non-Christians? Do we have anything in common? Of course we do. All people have certain basic needs and desires in common. According to psychologists, we all need food, water, clothing and shelter. Intangible needs include love and a sense of belonging (see Maslov's 1954 hierarchy of needs). However, Christians also have a desire to please God that the unsaved do not. Our desire to please God supersedes how we view our needs and desires. Although the lifestyles, motives and priorities of the saved and unsaved are usually different, humanity was created by God and in God's image. Once Christians understand and accept this basic commonality, we can gain a better appreciation for diversity.

However, it should be noted that although aspects of this book challenge readers to better understand and appreciate diversity, this challenge does not mean condoning every aspect of the beliefs and behavior of diverse cultures and groups simply because they are God's creation. As Christians, we are to rely on biblical standards as our moral and ethical guidelines to determine what is appropriate or inappropriate (in latter cases, appreciating diversity may simply reflect valuing the innate importance and value found in all living creatures or acknowledging the importance and value of an individual, while rejecting their behavior and beliefs). Thus, understanding the complexities of living in a diverse world also requires us to remember that, although everyone is God's *creation,* only those who accept Christ are considered God's *children.* I will discuss this issue in more detail in chapter three.

When I teach classes on sexuality and gender, many students are most interested in the topic of love. Although I present the topic from an academic approach, students are inevitably most interested in ways to apply the learning to their everyday lives. One study on love, by John Alan Lee (1974, 1977), is germane to this book. Based on interviews with scholars across disciplines such as literature, philosophy and the social sciences, and after reviewing thousands of statements regarding the subject of "love," Lee identifies six basic ways to love (which he calls "colors"). Interestingly enough, agape love is considered the highest form of love—and the most challenging. Lee found very few long-term agapic lovers. Although this form of love reflects selflessness, patience, altruism and reciprocity, he found that it only tends to be expressed episodically. Interestingly, in our relationships, people desire agape love, but often have difficulty showing it.[2] Given our society's tendency to encourage individualism, competition and mistrust,[3] it appears difficult to express agape love and to make oneself available to receive it. As Christians, we realize that expressing and receiving agape love is only possible as a result of a relationship with God through Jesus Christ.

Is it possible to love Jesus whom we have never seen and harbor prejudices against others we see every day? This appears to be a contradiction and impossibility. Christ tells us in John 14:15, "If you love me, you will keep my commandments." His greatest commandments were to love God totally *and* love others as we love ourselves (Mt 22:37-40). Scripture also states that we are "not to please ourselves" but "please our neighbor for the good purpose of building up the neighbor" (Rom 15:1-2). Following these guidelines shows our love and obedience to God. In order to accept others genuinely, it is necessary for Christians to refocus attention away from ourselves and toward God and others.

Have you ever noticed a group of children playing? The playgroup may consist of different nationalities, ethnicities, races, and both boys and girls but, in many cases, the children don't seem to notice. They can play happily and contentedly, unhampered by the societal weights brought on by adulthood and so-called maturity. A personal example also illustrates this point. One day while shopping, I entered a particularly crowded retail store. A white couple with several small children entered the store in front of me. Moving hurriedly, I ended up walking next to the couple's youngest child, who was about two years old. Thinking

---

[2]Lee's other colors include erotic, ludic (game-playing), storgic (companionate), manic and pragmatic loves. For additional information on styles of loving, refer to Lee 1974, 1977.

[3]Academic studies suggest increased focus on individualism, fears about group threats to perceived power, concerns about economic competition, and a growing "culture of victimization" in the United States (Blumer 1958; Etzioni 1991; Horowitz 1993; Jaret 1995; Marx [1848] 1977). A "me" ideology undermines the outward focus required for agape love.

that I was her mother, the little girl instinctively grabbed my hand. Several seconds later, she looked up at me and noticed that I indeed *was not* her mother. She stared at me peculiarly, eyes gleaming, but slightly bewildered. She knew that I was not her mother, but seemed unaware of the reason why. She was not afraid or upset, but merely looked around and, upon locating her mother, clasped her hand. Her mother and I laughed at what had happened. The innocence of that child touched me and further confirmed that we do not come into the world with prejudices or misconceptions about others who are different. In Matthew 18:3-4, we are encouraged to take the posture of a child in our approach to Christianity and in many other facets of our lives. We can learn a great deal from children. God loves and cares for us all and desires us to reciprocate that love to God and to others. God is not a respecter of persons and this provides the example for us to follow.

You may be saying, "Of course God can love and care for all people. God's perfect, but I am not!" It's true; all have sinned and come short of God's glory. However, this fact does not prevent us from striving to please God by emulating Christ. The biblical account of Peter's prejudices and subsequent change of heart as described in Acts 11 teaches how God views prejudices. God shows Peter that everyone is worthy of the opportunity to receive salvation. Peter's experience is an example of prejudices based on nationality/ethnicity and culture (Gentiles and Jews). This point is important to note, given the tendency to focus on race prejudice at the expense of other forms of prejudice that are often less apparent, but just as painful and *disempowering.

As Acts 11 unfolds, Peter's fellow Jewish friends, apostles and brethren alike, were concerned about his involvement with Gentiles (non-Jews). More specifically, Peter was witnessing to Gentiles and many were accepting Christ. Certain Jewish Christians felt that salvation was only available to them and that other groups were unclean and unacceptable. Peter had also supported this same philosophy until the Lord opened his eyes. In order to help his fellow Jewish friends, Peter described how the Lord, through a vision, had revealed his prejudices and challenged him to change. God made Peter understand that everything God made is inherently good, and furthermore, the gift of salvation is available to all.

Black Kids Sitting Together in the Cafeteria?). I know from experience.

I attended a predominantly male graduate school. The majority of students were white males from middle- or upper-class families. One articular class required a group project. Students began to gather in roups in various parts of the class to talk about tentative topics. I was vithout a group. As "the only" African American and one of few women n the class, previous experiences made me expect this. I asked several roups if they could use another partner, but they had enough. *I don't eed this rejection,* I thought. Sensing my difficulty, the professor laced me in a group. As the outsider, I was not usually accepted as a roup member. My ideas were squelched. My comments dismissed. ne male group member was openly hostile. I completed my project esponsibilities as quickly as possible and minimized my interaction ith the other group members.

The experience was so upsetting that I sought advice from a fellow udent who was African American. He was in the Ph.D. program and d been attending the school for over three years. Sadly, he did not of- r encouraging news. He had experienced similar treatment. According his observations, because we were African American, many white stu- nts did not believe we could contribute to a group effort. They as- med that we would be lazy freeloaders (*affirmative action babies) o would do little work but get the group grade. He advised me to try take classes that did not require group projects or to get special per- ssion from professors to complete projects alone. He also advised me "lie low" in classes and not to make waves; I would be sorry if I did. friend admitted that only the time and effort he had spent there made remain at such a racist institution. Female students often fared worse ing considered flighty, overly emotional or ill-equipped to under- nd science and math). And, as an African American female, I felt a ble whammy based on sex and race differences.

ut I do have something to offer! I thought. My background and job erience made me more knowledgeable about the topic than most of other project members. But because I was female and African Amer- , they assumed I didn't have anything significant to contribute to the rt. Because of their prejudices, the entire group lost. I lost out on the ortunity to participate in a more meaningful way; the other group

Prior to this revelation, even the great, bold apostle Peter had been unwilling to accept non-Jews! Upon the instruction of the Lord, he was compelled to break the existing Jewish tradition (a humanly made tenet) and preach the gospel to anyone who would listen. Peter's admission and submission to God's command represented a major change in his life, for he was agreeing to lay aside years of existing beliefs and inherent prejudices regarding Gentiles. I'm sure this was not an easy task for Peter, but, as a committed Christian, he could not say "no" to God. Peter went on to help save the souls of many Gentiles. Just as God did with Peter, the Lord will continue to uncover unacceptable attitudes, thoughts and behavior in our lives. Just as salvation is available to everyone, God can help us overcome prejudices in our lives when we are receptive and submissive, as Peter was, to God's will.

READ ABOUT

- **How God Feels About Humanity:** 1 John 4:7-12; John 3:16
- **How and Why Christians Are Related:** 1 Corinthians 12:13; Galatians 3:28; Romans 10:12
- **How to Treat Others:** Matthew 22:34-40

FOR PEACE

And even the hairs of your head are all counted.

MATTHEW 10:30

I was once riveted to my seat while watching a television show that featured a mother and child in a park. The mother was enjoying the park scenery while her baby innocently slept in a carriage that somehow began to move. As the carriage rolled, it picked up speed. The mother watched in horror as her child's carriage careened toward the street and into oncoming traffic. Instinctively, the mother raced into the traffic and pushed the carriage out of harm's way. The mother was not as fortunate, for she was struck by a car and killed.

God feels the same way about us. God protects us from hurt, harm and danger, blesses us and provides opportunities for growth and fulfillment. And God even made the ultimate sacrifice. As our heavenly parent, God always wants what's best for us. When we feel joy, God is joyful, and when we hurt, God hurts. God does not desire any of creation to hurt. But from time to time, we all do. Sometimes hurt comes as a result of things we do; hurt can also come as a result of things we should do, but don't. But sometimes others hurt us, not because of anything we've done, but based on their negative preconceived feelings, attitudes and beliefs about us—yes, prejudices.

Studies show that prejudicial attitudes and behavior are more common for some groups. In the United States, many people believe that the poor are lazy and lack motivation and discipline—although the majority of poor people work every day (Newman 1999; MacLeod 1995; NORC 1994; W. Wilson 1987, 1996). When racial differences in poverty are considered, studies show that although white poverty rates are lower than those of minorities, given their sheer number, there are more whites who are poor than minorities. Most African Americans are employed, and the majority of African Americans are not poor (Billingsley 1992). Poverty is disproportionately found among children, the "*working poor," and the elderly; a disproportionate percentage of African Americans and Hispanics are part of the former two groups. However, African Americans are more apt to experience prejudices based on stereotypes that associate them with poverty (Smith 1996; W. Wilson 1987, 1996). Although these findings are associated with race- and class-based prejudices and stereotypes, it appears that it is difficult to find a society without some form of prejudice.

Have you ever been on the receiving end of prejudices? If so, you probably remember that it was not a very good experience. A friend gave a personal example. Tina was always described as "very pretty . . . for an overweight woman." "If only she'd lose fifty pounds," they'd say. People admired her hourglass figure (plump women also have figures, you know), flawless skin and bubbly personality. Everyone got along with Tina. Few realized her feelings of isolation and sadness and lack of peace. Tina was the only "plump" person in her group of friends. If they went out for an evening of dancing, she could usually be found at the table, watching the coats and refreshments as her friends danced the night away. Men just seemed to overlook her. *They have to see me. How could they not!* Tina mused cynically. But no matter where they went or what they did, men did not seem to be interested in Tina. If by

chance she did start a conversation with a man, he would in
gin to ask her about one of her thinner friends. Sometimes
his pal or best buddy, but she was not viewed as a potent
interest. Years and years of rejection have caused Tina to be
sive. Now, on the rare occasion when she does go out with
sits silently, afraid to talk with men for fear of the inevitab
Tina's experience reminds us that it is possible to hold subt
against large-sized people and others often considered less
though Tina felt alone in her predicament, it is a common
societies that emphasize physical features and an idealiz
beauty (a topic I will discuss in more detail in chapter five

"The only!" It's no fun being "the only." This phrase ca
describe a person who is somehow different from a gr
they're a part. They're often treated differently from othe
bers. Being "the only" can bring about feelings of isolation
moil.[4] Personal peace is often difficult to attain when you
Have you ever been the only woman in a college course?
in a department? The only single person at a couples-orie
The only Christian at a job outing? The only freshman in a
lege class? The only Asian in a project group? The only p
a group? Most of us have probably been "the only" at
lives. But can you imagine being "the only" most the tim
makes matters worse if you are "the only" and face prejuc
it. What can Tina do? How should she act? Should she
Or maybe find some plump friends? Why should Tina ha
she's happy and healthy, why should others make her
Some persons might be concerned for Tina for health
because of negative feelings based on images of the "
Some people may be distant or leery of "the only" pe
mistrust or ignorance. Others are purposefully indiff
mean based on prejudices (see Beverly Tatum's [1999

[4]Tajfel (1982) discusses some of the psychological implications of in-gr
namics.

[5]Refer to Wellman and Friedberg (2002) and Rippe (1996) on obesity a
ages of ideal body sizes have been used to devalue larger-sized per
here is reflective of the process of observation or description [i.e., so
than others or are taller and have larger frames than others] and not

members lost out on the benefit of my expertise. The experience left me feeling dejected, isolated and depressed. After several similar experiences, I wanted to have very little to do with any part of *that* school! What was wrong with *those* students? They seemed to be trapped in the old South mentality. Hadn't they been exposed to women and other minorities who did not fit their stereotypical image?[6] If they had, it obviously hadn't made a difference. And why did I feel so isolated? Why did I feel so *different* from other students? Maybe I should just transfer to another school—because all *these* students don't like women and they certainly don't care for African Americans!

These and other questions raced through my mind as I attempted to reconcile my school experiences. Each *minority group, the few that were there, seemed to have found its own way to cope with campus life. Asians studied and interacted primarily with other Asians, African Americans with African Americans, and Mexican Americans with Mexican Americans. The few white female students associated primarily with white males. The few minority women who attended the school seemed to scramble for friendship and study partners wherever they could be found. As I was generally "the only" African American and "the only" female in most classes, my isolation, sadness and turmoil was renewed with each course that I took.

Patricia Hill Collins (2000) vividly describes this feeling of being an outsider and suggests that a careful examination of experiences based on race, class and gender reveals common evidence of how excluded groups often experience life and see themselves. Collins suggests that these types of *oppression are interconnected because outsider groups experience varying amounts of penalties and privileges based on their relative positions in society. Using her own experiences as the point of departure, she suggests that outsiders often lose their "voices" and become silenced as they attempt to interact among other groups that devalue and subordinate them. Outsiders are made to feel smaller and less

---

[6]Readers are encouraged to examine the groundbreaking studies on racial stereotypes by Katz and Braly (1933) and on class and race stereotypes by Smedley and Bayton (1978). MacDonald (1992) examines stereotypes about minorities in general. Other stereotypes characterize the poor as lazy and irresponsible (NORC 1996); men as dominant, intelligent and insensitive; and women as overly emotional, irrational and helpless (Bem 1981, 1993).

important and may begin to view themselves in less favorable terms due to negative ideas, attitudes and expectations, which Collins describes as "controlling images." She suggests that controlling images are designed to make racism, sexism and poverty appear natural, normal and inevitable. She contends that such images can also keep women oppressed and maintain interlocking systems of race, class and gender oppression. For Collins, the controlling images of others negatively affect how outsiders may view life. Collins's assessment described my situation perfectly.

But this just doesn't make sense, I thought. *We're all rational, logical human beings*. But try as I might, I could not reconcile my peers' attitudes and behavior and my ever-growing tendency to isolate myself. *I can't win,* I thought. *I can't (and don't want to) change who I am—and others* can *and won't change their attitudes and behavior.* Because I was continually rejected and ignored, I attempted to reject and ignore those who made me feel rejected and ignored. I was trapped in a vicious cycle of prejudice! Although we sat in class together, the chasm between my fellow students and me was enormous. It also seemed unlikely that we would ever make "contact." Seeking support was not an option. The few minority school officials, themselves in powerless positions, would listen to my plight but were unable to provide help. "Just stick it out," they'd say, "for the good of our people."

And stick it out I did.

My parents always encouraged us children to "finish what you start." Despite the obstacles, I was determined to graduate. But I needed peace to be victorious; I sought spiritual guidance. Although I had been praying, studying my Bible and fellowshiping with a church throughout my ordeal, I knew it was necessary to intensify my spiritual support in order to not just endure but to understand what God wanted me to learn from the experience and to thrive. Above all, I wanted to again have peace in my life.

I told close friends from church of my ordeal and asked for their prayers. I sought Scripture for answers to the many questions that plagued me. One Scripture in particular served as inspiration: "If God be for us, who can be against us?" (Rom 8:31 KJV). The Holy Spirit continually brought this passage to my remembrance. I was God's child. I remembered my childhood with Christian parents: my faith in them, how they took care of me, their ability to help, even when I didn't realize it, the peace in knowing that Mom and Dad were there for me. God had promised to do so much more. I decided to tap into the peace that was available to me as God's child. Lastly, I relinquished the entire situation to God. Why worry about it—God was in control! God gradually began to restore my peace.

Interestingly, although an academic endeavor, findings from Pat Hill Collins's study also parallel ways in which godly peace and new resolve can be attained. She encourages outsiders to embrace a "self-definition"—going outside traditional definitions and symbols imposed by others to define oneself. And the three elements of her challenge involve (and affect) self-reliance, self-esteem and independence and help persons reject controlling images. In the same manner that I sought refuge, Collins also illustrates how the traditional black church service, in general, and the *call-and-response tradition in particular have been used by African American women to build community and create and maintain a more positive sense of self.[7]

Like a child who is totally dependent on his or her parents, God required my total dependence. The situation was too much for me to handle. As a child, I remember constantly saying "my daddy said this" or "my momma did that" in reference to my confidence in my earthly parents. My earthly mother and father were true to their word—God would be as well. God had a proven *track record* in the past; I could expect the same now. I wasn't sure exactly *how* the situation would be resolved, only that God would work through the situation and through me to make everything okay. I continued to study and complete my coursework. If I did my part, God would do the rest. The more I relied on God, the more peace I experienced. (For other helpful suggestions refer to Schuller [1993] *Power Thoughts;* Bloomfield [1986] *Making Peace with Yourself;* and Nouwen [1989] *Lifesigns: Intimacy, Fecundity, and Ecstasy in Christian Perspective.*) I was also determined to reach out to my fellow classmates. I knew that they *all* weren't prejudiced. As in Matthew

[7]According to Collins (2000) other ways to combat controlling images include forging relationships with other persons who have been treated negatively and feel like outsiders, the African American women's blues tradition, and reading the work of African American women writers who offer alternative self-definitions.

13:24-30, the wheat and tares were simply in class together. I started searching for wheat! Although it was difficult initially and some students were unresponsive, in each class, I began to meet genuinely nice people—some were Christians, some were not. I specifically recall two white male classmates with whom I became good friends. My level of peace and spiritual resolve were becoming stronger.

You may be thinking, *But it's so hard when you're "the only."* During my last semester in this same graduate program, a group project was again required for a class. Again, I was without a group. Again, the professor placed me in a group. Again, the leery stares and strained interaction. After we chose our project topic, various group members began to suggest possible approaches. I too, made a suggestion; it went unheeded. Not this time, I promised myself. As the discussion continued, I continued to make comments and remarks. Despite rejection, I made my opinions heard, my expertise known. It was obvious that I was not going to be dismissed or ignored. This time, I would remain undaunted.

As I interacted more closely with the group, I was reminded that, regardless of their attitudes and acts, they too were God's creation. We had things in common and our commonalities often outweighed our differences. It appeared that I was "the only," but we all wanted to graduate from school, enjoy college, make friends, meet people and find good jobs. We were all also dealing with grade anxieties, competition and the many other challenges of campus life. And for many of these students, I was their first close contact with an African American female. However, for those who continued to harbor racial prejudice, that was their problem, not mine.[8]

Part of finding peace was remembering my worth and maintaining my position as a valuable, informed student, capable of learning and contributing. As the group progressed and we got to know each other, the strain eased. Each member volunteered for certain tasks. Despite the very vocal objections of a white female member, I was selected group leader. The project was a success for reasons other than our grade of A.

[8]However, the reader should note the differences in addressing and negotiating around prejudices among peers as compared to the additional problems if those in positions of authority over you (i.e., supervisor or instructor) harbor prejudices and if prejudices and discrimination are institutionalized (Collins 2000; Hayes 2000; Omi and Winant 1994; West 1993).

I was able to reconcile my status as "the only" as a reality to be appreciated, even when others did not. My peace was renewed. I didn't attain peace from the group members or from their feelings about me or actions toward me, but from God. And even now if I feel like "the only," I am never alone. God and I make the majority!

READ ABOUT

- **God's Help:** Psalms 9:9; 22:19; Hebrews 4:14-16
- **God's Provisions:** Matthew 7:7-12; John 16:33

3

Some Reasons Prejudices Exist

FOR POWER

Search me, O God, and know my heart;
test me and know my thoughts. . . .
and lead me in the way everlasting.
PSALM 139:23-24

In this Scripture David asked the Lord to examine him, to delve deep into his heart and thoughts. I'm sure David knew that when God searched him, he would probably uncover areas that needed to be improved. This would require David to change. But David also knew that spiritual growth toward "the way everlasting" would result. Like David, Christian growth results from *self-reflection and making changes as we grow spiritually.

Contrary to popular belief, we don't effectively learn about diverse groups in general through the media. Information on television or radio can be limited or distorted (Dennis and Pease 1997). And prejudice is often fueled by lack of knowledge. When we know little about people, we may make assumptions that may or may not be true.

Research shows a cyclic relationship that can exist between prejudice and discrimination (Macionis 1999). In Stage 1, prejudice and discrimination begin by inaccurately judging another person or group using yourself or group as the standard (called *ethnocentrism). At this stage, prejudice is usually used to justify taking advantage of the devalued person or group. In Stage 2, prejudice and exploitation result in the devalued person or group being considered socially inferior. And in Stage 3, the problems experienced by the devalued person or group that *actually* resulted from prejudice and discrimination are considered *evidence* that the person or group is inferior and justifies continued prejudice and discrimination. In such a cycle, prejudice and subsequent discrimination based on factors such as race, sexual orientation, sex, religion, ethnicity, nationality and class become the motivation *and* outcome.

Prejudice usually involves pigeon holing people based on limited or lack of exposure or on things we've heard or seen—even though we all know that things are seldom *black and white*. Here's an example: a certain fitness commercial aired on television. The woman in the commercial was physically fit, muscular and toned. During the commercial she gives several helpful hints to get into shape. Her last hint is, "Stop eating like a pig and you'll lose weight." Initially I didn't think much about the commercial. Later on I thought about the possible message it sent to viewers about themselves and others. Think about it: Sally is overweight; overweight people eat like pigs; therefore Sally must eat like a pig because she is overweight. Although this is a somewhat simple example, it illustrates how prejudices can develop. It is sometimes easy to come to a conclusion based on limited information, but if that conclusion is based on incomplete or incorrect information, the conclusion is faulty.

Sweeping generalities often feed prejudices and can result in entrenched views or behavior of which we may not even be aware. You might think that this example is far-fetched, but you can't imagine the number of times in my business travels and personal relationships that I've been told that I don't act, talk or behave like an "African American" or that I think "like a man." I wonder, *just how does an African American act, talk and behave? How does a man think?* It would be easy if there was a *typical* African American or a *typical* single person or a *typical* Asian American or a *typical* male or a *typical* poor person. These types of far-fetched (and insensitive, I might add) comments can be linked to the continued existence of prejudices.

I contend that addressing forms of prejudices in society will help persons better understand, acknowledge and possibly appreciate the diversity found in humanity. However, it is important to also remember the overarching biblical dictates that should guide the lives and moral and ethical decisions made by Christians. Some examples of biblical mandates that should shape our lives include keeping God first in our lives (Mt 6:33; 22:37-38), loving our neighbor as ourselves (Mt 22:39-40) and practicing attitudes and actions motivated by love (Mt 5:43-44; 1 Cor 13). The ability to acknowledge and, when appropriate, appreciate diversity can be complicated for Christians because we are called to follow biblical dictates for acceptable and unacceptable attitudes and behavior. Thus although we may acknowledge group differences and recognize their existence as seemingly rational outcomes for a particular group, we are also challenged to evaluate them based on biblical standards.

For example, although we may understand the impetus and cultural history of *female genital mutilation that occurs in parts of Africa and Asia, these beliefs and customs are considered contrary to Christianity and should be rejected (and fought against) by Christians. Similarly and even more potentially complex, cultural practices informed by *biblical* interpretations that suggest "children should be seen and not heard" or "the poor will always be with us" can result in abuse, oppression, neglect and other forms of mistreatment of children and the poor. These types of attitudes and actions should be questioned by Christians, and part of our ministry should combat these social problems. However, readers should also note that such persons or groups should not be dismissed *en masse* because of biblically offensive attitudes or practices; they may possess other traits to be acknowledged or appreciated—and they are capable of change.

The challenge to address prejudices and appreciate others should not be interpreted as blanket acceptance or affirmation of all forms of diversity or a call to ignore individual or group differences that are offensive, dangerous or that conflict with biblical mandates. Rather, we are challenged to value individuals and groups, become better informed regarding cultural differences, and use discernment to determine whether our views about diverse groups are rooted in prejudices. In this chapter, I focus on common factors that can result in prejudices that limit power and five factors relative to peace, as well as some consequences of prejudices for our lives and Christian testimony. The overall goal is to examine subjects that research suggests are linked to the perpetuation of prejudices among bearers and continued prejudicial experiences on the part of recipients. As in earlier chapters, I consider the implications of the existence of prejudices for bearers first, followed by an examination of similar dynamics for recipients.

Prejudice and Ethnocentrism

Earlier I mentioned the possible link between ethnocentrism and prejudice. Every society has standards by which citizens live. Those standards considered most important often become laws (for example, against marrying underaged persons, against stealing and murder). In other instances standards are reflected in norms and values. Standards can change, because what a society considers acceptable or unacceptable may change (for example, the age for marital consent varies by state). To complicate matters further, groups within a given society may have their own set of norms and values that may coincide or conflict with those of other groups.

Ethnocentrism occurs when we use the standards of our group to evaluate another group unfavorably. Let's consider an example using two churches, one "Pentecostal" and the other "Conservative." It would be ethnocentric if members of the Pentecostal church suggested that the worship service at the Conservative church was somehow less authentic or suspect because the latter group did not, say, speak in tongues, stand and clap during choral selections or say "Amen" during the sermon. Such a belief would mean that Pentecostalism was the standard, benchmark or measure by which other churches should be evaluated. Because both churches are Christian communities, differences in worship services may simply reflect different styles of praising God (i.e., different church cultures). Instead, it is important to be *culturally relative,* meaning that we acknowledge and appreciate diversity.[1] *Cultural relativity is best expressed everyday by acknowledging and understanding cultural differences (food, clothing, language, hairstyles, values, practices), even though they differ from our own.

Similar to my comments earlier in this chapter, issues of rejecting ethnocentrism and embracing cultural relativity must be biblically informed

[1]The reader should again note that my challenge toward cultural relativity does not mean automatically accepting everything from other cultures (or our own, for that matter) or condoning cultural differences that go against biblical dictates. Scripture is the standard for attitudes and conduct.

for Christians because we rely on the Bible to make decisions. Thus my challenge to avoid ethnocentrism is not to encourage acceptance of all forms of diversity, but rather a call to value humanity, to become more culturally aware and to realize the possible relationship between certain forms of ethnocentrism and prejudices. Broadly speaking, we are challenged to avoid ethnocentrism that undermines the inherent value found in others. The type of ethnocentrism I am challenging readers to avoid is often rooted in feelings of superiority, false pride and over-confidence. I learned this lesson the hard way.

I was valedictorian of my high school class. I was very proud of this fact since I had always taken a full course load of college preparatory classes. My family was also proud since I was the first valedictorian in the family. What an accomplishment! I was not walking on cloud nine, but on cloud twelve! Just think, I had earned better grades than all my other classmates. To add to this accomplishment, I had done so while holding the student council presidency. That was a major feat indeed. During the months after graduation, I began to change. No, I did not turn into a beast that walked around bragging and putting other people down. The change was very subtle—I was jumping back and forth across the line between healthy pride and conceit. I found myself less patient with others if I understood things more quickly than they. I was silently amused at the simple mistakes of others since I, of course, would never do such things. When involved in church and school activities, very seldom did I allow others to lead. I knew that they could do a good job, but I could do better.

Since the change was so subtle, if you did not know me well, you probably would not have even guessed that my attitude was different. However, as time went on, my conceit grew. Only those persons who were as smart as *I thought I was* or outstanding in some area could get my respect. I had established a standard to evaluate others—based on grades and "intellect"—and most people fell short. I had become "ethnocentric." Of course God did not allow this to last long. I had exalted myself too much and for the wrong reasons and, as Luke 14:11 says, I had to be humbled. God allowed me to go through certain experiences to humble me. The first humbling experience took place when I went to college. There I met hundreds of students who were just as smart and just as well rounded as I was. And when I made A's in classes, so did most of the other students. When I excelled, I was never alone. Some students even made better grades than I did—and with less effort! Many of my college classmates were bright, but I also noticed that most of them were not conceited. Most took their gifts in stride. There was a genuine desire to help other people and a strong feeling of friendship. I was impressed with this—and ashamed of what I had become.

There were also students who had other talents besides making A's. The campus was full of artists, musicians, writers, orators, some of whom might never make the "A honor roll," but who had gifts that were just as valuable and just as important as mine. God's message was quite clear to me: everyone has something to offer and God establishes the standard by which humanity is evaluated—not me. This experience caused me to take a good hard look at myself. I had created criteria (based on grades) by which I accepted and respected others. Because of "ethnocentrism," my classmates' value had been reduced to grade point averages, exam results and quiz points. Honest, consistent introspection revealed this area in which I needed growth. Looking inside ourselves can be quite painful, but is often the only way to uncover areas that we need to change. Attitudes and beliefs (things inside us) can result in a lack of understanding of others, and a feeling of superiority can engender prejudices and possibly discrimination. However, studies show that some of the most powerful factors that result in various forms of prejudice occur both *inside* and *outside* oneself.

Prejudice and Groupthink

The term *atypical* is an understatement when used to compare Jesus to the spiritual leaders of his day. Those around him could not understand most of his actions and motives. On occasion, even the disciples were stumped by a word he said or deed he performed. Jesus was unique in his approach to those around him. He did not attempt to stand out for the sake of being seen or admired by others. He stood out because his actions paralleled his message. As the old folks would say, Jesus didn't just talk the Christian talk, but he walked the godly walk. In some instances, we may find ourselves succumbing to group pressure and accepting prejudices or taking part in prejudicial activities. *Groupthink refers to the tendency to conform to the opinions and behavior of group members when alone we probably would think and do differently. When people experience groupthink, they are often more interested in pleasing the group (even when the group is wrong) and are less likely to oppose group decisions (Janis 1972).

The story of the woman with the alabaster jar in Luke 7 is one example of how Jesus rejected groupthink and showed that he was different. As the passage unfolds, a woman of questionable character approaches Christ and his companions as they prepare to dine. She carries an expensive jar of perfume and washes and perfumes Christ's feet. Because most travel was done on foot over dusty roads, foot washing was a common practice. However, tradition also dictated that women of ill repute should be avoided. Some of his disciples and the other guests wanted the woman to leave. Imagine how Christ might have reacted had he given in to pressure from the group. He might have ignored the woman and her genuine attempts to show reverence. He might have joined the judgmental throng and rejected her because of her past. He might have made a few "politically correct" remarks to the woman and quickly sent her on her way. He might have blindly accepted tradition as just the way things are and asked her to leave. Or he might have done nothing—frozen by the fear of all possible outcomes. But Christ did not fear going against group sentiment. Not only did he allow her to remain in his presence, Christ allowed her to touch him! This action was shocking to those who only saw it from an earthly perspective. However, Jesus was able to see more than her physical gesture.

Many other biblical examples can be given of Jesus choosing to think and act differently and associating with people who were considered common or different by society. He was comfortable with the rich and the poor, with the saved as well as the unsaved (he was most interested in the latter group). His friendliness was not out of pity or patronizing acts of indifference, but due to concern and love. He saw each person as a unique individual of value and he genuinely cared about each one—no matter what those around him said or thought. What would you have done if you had been confronted by the woman with the alabaster jar? Does God dictate your actions and beliefs or are you overly influenced by groups to which you belong? Have you had the opportunity to interact with those who are different from you, those shunned by society or persons considered socially unacceptable, but failed to do so because of groupthink? We are often confronted with the desire to fit in and please others. Peer pressure can be difficult. It is often easier to go along with the crowd than to dare to be different. Many Christians may have the desire to stand up and speak out against prejudices and injustices but are hindered by groupthink. As Christians, pleasing God is our primary purpose. Being different may require us to interact with and possibly forge relationships with those who are different from us.

Prejudice and Aversive Racism

Is it possible to harbor prejudices and not be aware of them? According to research on prejudice, discrimination and racism by Samuel Gaertner and John Dovidio (1986) traditional forms of racism have been replaced by more subtle, less obvious forms of bigotry. This recent phenomena, which they refer to as *aversive racism, suggests that persons do not hold consistently negative or positive attitudes about minorities, but are, in fact, ambivalent. Unlike racists who openly display racial intolerance, aversive racists typically hold strong egalitarian beliefs and express sympathy for the victims of injustices. They are also likely to support, in principle, public policy that promotes racial equality and adhere to a more liberal political stance. Aversive racists would not consider themselves prejudiced, may not be aware of their racist beliefs and attitudes, and go to great lengths to mask their prejudices. Intolerance by aversive racists generally manifests itself in the form of discomfort, uneasiness, disgust, fear (all attitudes and beliefs) and, ultimately, avoidance (behavior) of minority groups. Because aversive racists may not be aware of their prejudices, the authors support the need for laws that provide checks-and-balances against possible discrimination. Applying Gaertner and Dovidio's findings in other contexts, it can be argued that prejudices can result in aversions to other groups in society that we may be sympathetic toward in theory (for example, the poor), but avoid in practice. (Also refer to Apostle, Glock, Piazza and Suelzle's [1983] *The Anatomy of Racial Attitudes;* and McConahay 1983.)

Prejudice and Fear of Rejection

Fear of rejection represents another potential stumbling block to addressing prejudices and acknowledging or embracing others. You may have been rejected when you tried to reach out to someone in the past and you don't want it to happen again. But they may have good reasons for being skeptical. They may have been skeptical about your motives. Past experiences may have made them leery, even though you had the best of intentions (Roediger 1991). No one wants to be rejected as he or she attempts to make a gesture of friendship. Although we tend to take rejection personally, it is usually not a direct reflection on us. When we open up to others and they do not respond in a way that we desire, our natural reaction is to shy away from similar future encounters. Uncertainty about the outcome of an event (especially if one of the possible outcomes could be negative) often hinders us from getting involved. Although it may be difficult, Christians are challenged to reach out to others, even at the risk of being rejected. Initial rejection does not mean that our words or actions have been in vain. God honors our genuine efforts to reach out to others—even when we are not embraced in return. Our effort may also be one of many that is needed to bring about positive change in the hearts and actions of others. This change may occur in the future, when we aren't around to witness it. Showing love in the face of rejection will also change our lives as God gives us added courage, strength and boldness. We are encouraged to plant seeds for Christ even if we are not around to see the final harvest.

Prejudice and Fear of Alienation

Most of my immediate family and friends are Christians, attend church regularly and are involved in church activities. My parents were devout Christians; my father was a deacon and trustee; my mother was a Sunday school teacher, choir director and church secretary. My older sister was the Sunday school secretary, and I became the church pianist at age twelve. As far back as I can remember, Christ has been a major part of my life. I cannot imagine anything different. How would it have felt to grow up in a home that was not headed by Christian parents? How would it have felt not to have Christian sisters and friends or to have negative, ungodly family members?

Becky was not part of a Christian family; childhood memories were of fights, substance abuse, poverty and pain. As an adult she gave her life to Christ and has since been blessed spiritually and in other areas of her life. Yet her old friends and family members are still unsaved and seem to be trapped in a cycle of self-destruction, hopelessness and death. She calls them frequently but seldom goes home because it hurts her to see their condition. She has told them about Christ and how he changed her life. Their replies have been taunts and slurs—"holy roller," "goody two shoes," "Jesus freak"—and accusations: "You're not saved. I remember you when . . ." Not only do they deny Jesus and attempt to undermine her relationship with him, they also reject Becky's desire to reach out to and minister to other racial and ethnic groups, most of whom they consider inferior.[2] Would your family reject you if your best friend were Asian? Would they question your decision to date a less educated man? Would they look down on you for attending a predominately Hispanic church? How would they react to your "overweight" fiancée? Would they eye your friend from the "wrong side of the tracks" suspiciously? Each of us may face being ostracized by family, acquaintances and friends who may hold rigid, negative views of others and seek to limit our relationships. It is often difficult to jeopardize existing relationships for people we do not know personally or understand. Christ requires us to be willing to, if need be, sacrifice earthly relationships for divine purposes.

Prejudice and Personal Frailties

Have you ever heard some variation of the following statements, "I thought you said you were a Christian? You're supposed to be so holy" or "If Christians act like that, I'm glad to be a sinner"? Comments like these can cause us to place unnecessary pressure on ourselves and fellow Christians to meet some secular standard of Christian living. It is uncomfortable to admit shortcomings (and on-lookers may not make it any easier). However, God knows that we are imperfect. God wants us to admit shortcomings to ourselves and ask for help to overcome them. Not only will the Lord provide strength to overcome our frailties, but others

---

[2]Refer to Adorno's (1950) research on authoritarian personalities who hold bigoted views, in general, about minority groups.

can help too (strong Christians are to help the weak, as described in Rom 15:1). It is easier to ignore prejudice than to confront it. Confronting it may mean discovering our own prejudices. It may mean opening up a Pandora's box of emotions, feelings, beliefs and actions that are not in line with Christ's teachings and go against the Christian image many of us try to present. Many may wonder, how would church members react to a pastor who is prejudiced against a particular group? Would parents allow me to teach their children Sunday school if they knew how I felt about "those people"? How would my Christian testimony be affected if others discovered my prejudices against "that group"?

Sociologist Erving Goffman (1959) uses theater imagery to explain and describe day-to-day interactions. According to Goffman, as we interact with others, each of us attempts to present the best (idealized) image of "self." We strive to insure that we act "the part" we are attempting to present to others (referred to as "front stage")—all while working to minimize the ability of others to see those things we think and do that may undermine this created and well-crafted presentation of ourselves (referred to as "back stage"). Using his analysis relative to this book, back stage can refer to prejudices and discrimination that we believe will undermine our Christian testimony. But even if we are able to hide these frailties from others, we can't hide them from God, and they stymie *empowered living. Fear of showing frailties can prevent us from acknowledging our prejudices. Yes, admitting our frailties may give others something to gossip about. But admitting frailties also frees us from fear so that we can work to improve. Prejudices cannot be changed unless they are first acknowledged. Each of us has and will continue to have areas in our lives where spiritual growth is needed, and we should not attempt to hide these areas for fear of the opinions of others. A relationship with Christ is personal, but it should also be manifested publicly as we show evidence of this relationship in our attitudes and behavior. Prejudices undermine such endeavors.

Prejudice and "the Other"

One day while at work I had an interesting conversation with a white male coworker. He and I had become friends and often talked of like interests. On this particular day, our usual conversation shifted to an unusual incident. He described how he became uncomfortable when he saw African American men wearing paraphernalia of the civil rights leader Malcolm X. My coworker further explained that, although he did not fully understand why he became nervous, it had continued to bother him. He felt somehow threatened by these men. I asked him whether the men had approached him or harassed him in any way; he responded in the negative. I went on to ask other questions, trying to delve deeper and better understand his concerns. It appeared that his fear was based on the unknown. He didn't know what the men meant by wearing the paraphernalia. Knowing that Malcolm X had at one time preached hatred, were the men saying that they hated whites? Unknowingly, my coworker had objectified the men he had encountered. He did not consider them to be individuals, but rather as a potentially dangerous group. Objectification involves lumping people into one large category, believing them to be dramatically different from us ("the Other") and then behaving differently toward them (in this case, my friend's attempt to distance himself from them).

As we continued to talk, I thought it interesting that he (and some other whites) feel uneasy about a historical figure that is esteemed by many African Americans. It also concerned me that he was afraid and that his fear might hinder future relationships with African American males. I went on to explain that he had not been in danger. Only his preconceived notions caused him to believe the men meant him harm. I challenged him to read about the life and experiences of Malcolm X as a way of humanizing and personalizing him (Haley 1973). I challenged my friend to try not to judge people based on outward appearances. Long after I had forgotten about our conversation, my coworker told me that my comments had made a difference in his outlook. Just as my friend did, we may develop preconceived ideas about "the Other" that can foster prejudices and stereotypes. We are cautious because we aren't sure what to expect, and unfortunately we often expect the worse. It then becomes easier to avoid people who differ from us than to face our concerns.

Prejudice and the Media

We are bombarded daily by media representations that directly and indirectly influence our attitudes and behavior. Television, radio, print media and the Internet have enabled us to establish networks and relationships globally. Despite the benefits of the media, it is important to examine ways in which the media may promote and perpetuate prejudices. In their book *The Media in Black and White* Everette Dennis and Edward C. Pease (1997) examine the role of the media in promoting negative images in society. They claim that in order to generate profit and improve ratings, the media often feeds on preexisting stereotypes and fears of the audience by presenting what people *expect* to see (for example, minorities and poor people as criminals) or titillating the audience. Similarly, Erving Goffman (1979)[3] reviewed newspaper and magazine ads to examine differences in ways men and women are presented. His findings revealed subtle biases in media representations based on gender, where men were usually presented as superior, competent and having authority, and women were conveyed in submissive roles. These two studies do not suggest that all media representations engender prejudices, but rather that the media has been prone to present stereotypical images that may influence our ability to objectively view others.

Prejudice and Competition

The American dream—success, economic stability, a comfortable life, a happy family, a nice car and a beautiful home (S. Barnes and Jaret 2003; Newman 1988, 1993)—is a philosophy central to our society, and most people strive to get their piece of the "American pie." Many of us are also taught that the American pie is only so big—if you get more, others get less. Likewise, when others prosper, they do so at your expense. Most people accept a certain amount of competition. Some people are afraid of too much competition or of competition from certain groups of people. Concerns about competition for jobs, wealth and positions in top schools for our children have been shown to create tensions among disparate groups (Marx [1848] 1977; Newman 1988; Wilson 1987).

Sociological studies on the movement of the hate group known as the Skinheads confirm what we already knew—most Skinheads hate minor-

---

[3]Goffman's work also showed that men were often portrayed as clumsy, ill-prepared and unsuccessful when doing traditional women's work such as babysitting, cooking or laundry.

ities. Research also uncovered that many Skinheads hate minorities because they believe that minorities have taken away jobs that should belong to white people. They blame the economic conditions of many poor whites on a lack of jobs—jobs that have been given (they believe) to minorities. This form of *scapegoating enables persons to vent their anger and frustration on others, usually similarly economically less empowered groups. In this way, minority groups can become the target of scapegoating and can be unfairly blamed for problems others face (Blumer 1958; Dollard 1939).

Many may fear competition from groups who were not able or not allowed to compete with them for economic, political and social positions and influence in the past. Minorities, women, immigrants—these groups are now competing for a "piece of the pie" in larger numbers than in the past. Some people may have never imagined that they would have to compete with members of these groups for positions, power and privileges. "She was given *my* job because of affirmative action" or "These foreigners are taking over the country." These statements reflect prejudicial beliefs toward the many diverse hands that now want their share of the American pie. Prejudices often appear as a backlash of fear of competition. Fear of competition can result in our considering other persons or groups to be the enemy or obstacles to our share of success. Who created this American pie anyway? Why are people so concerned about getting a piece of it? Why does it have so few pieces? As Christians, we are reminded that God owns the cattle on a thousand hills (Ps 50:10). Fear of competition can result in preoccupation with earthly pursuits as well as justification for prejudicial attitudes and behavior to "get our fair share."

Prejudice and Hierarchies

Most societies have both well-established and tacit hierarchies. What is a *hierarchy and how can it be linked to possible prejudices? Hierarchies can be defined as rankings or classifications of persons or groups based on some socially accepted criteria. Such rankings are usually based on economic or social standing; other times hierarchies are established based on perceived group ability, professional status or access to power. Certain rankings make sense (e.g., that adults are responsible for children and thus make major decisions for them until they mature). Others seem to be accepted without question and can lead to feelings of superiority and possible prejudices. Here is an example.

Due to a recent series of travels, I found myself in airports quite a bit, where I was reminded of a widely accepted hierarchy based on economic position (or class). First-class and business-class fliers are given priority during almost every phase of a trip: at check-in, when boarding, even when deplaning. During flights a curtain is usually closed between the first-class compartment to separate it from coach (i.e., a reminder of the hierarchy). Persons in the premier area on the plane are given better (and more) food and beverages and have more restrooms per passenger than those in coach. It just seems illogical to me to have, say, four restrooms for 125 coach passengers and four restrooms for 15 first-class and business-class passengers (and coach customers cannot use the restrooms in first class, even if they are not in use). Even the title (first class or premier class) reflects this hierarchy. During a recent flight, the possible implications of this type of hierarchy became evident.

The airport experienced severe delays due to bad weather; this resulted in extremely long check-in lines. However, airline representatives responsible for checking in first-class customers were unable to also assist in the process for the rest of us—even when there were no first-class customers to check in and the coach line was almost trailing out the door! Again this seemed illogical to me—especially as I watched the many elderly people and folks with small children waiting in the coach line. I was traveling light so I didn't feel too put upon (except for the illogic of the situation), but I felt sorry for other coach passengers who were having a hard time in the long line and could not be "assisted" simply because they had not purchased high-priced tickets. My comments, of course, do not mean that I am unaware of how airlines make profit and why they are in business. (I know first-class and business-class customers pay significantly more for this special treatment and are the mainstays of airline travel.) However, some of the effects of airline hierarchies can suggest a certain level of entitlement. Let's get back to my story.

The flight was eventually canceled and we were given hotel vouchers to spend the night—several hundred people were affected. When waiting in line (yet again) at the hotel, I was several persons behind a young man who appeared to be a college student (book bag, headphones, baseball cap, T-shirt, jeans—I assumed he was in college rather than high school because he was traveling alone). He was in front of an older man who, by his dress, luggage and computer bag, appeared to be a businessperson. The older man began to complain loudly about the long lines; he stated that he had a reservation at the hotel and should not have to wait behind all the people who did not. He ranted about the money that he would be spending for the hotel stay. His comments and tone suggested a clear sense of entitlement based on his perceived class or economic position and the expectation that he should be able to get in line ahead of everyone else. The student calmly but immediately responded. He said that everyone had had a difficult, long day at the airport and that we were all trying to deal with a bad situation. However, he stated, if the older man felt that he was better than the rest of us, he (the student) would be happy to give him (the older man) his place in line. It became quiet. Everyone looked at the older man and the student—and waited. I smiled. The older man simply put his head down and waited quietly in line.

I was pleased to witness how the young man respectfully challenged the older man to reconsider his classist attitude. The older man seemed to believe that because he had been given preferential treatment at the airport (and probably in many other arenas in his life), he should get special treatment at the hotel.[4] He thought that he was somehow more entitled than everyone else in line (i.e., classism and elitism). The young man was discerning enough to question him and, in doing so, reminded me of the importance of continually questioning and challenging hierarchies and their possible correlation to prejudices. The experience also encouraged me because of the burgeoning wisdom and action-oriented nature of a young man who was not afraid to speak up for what he believed.

Consequences of Unaddressed Prejudices

Sometimes Christians are quiet about the injustices that take place around us. It is often easy to simply ignore or downplay prejudices. Remember Lot and his experiences in the city of Sodom in Genesis 19? Lot decided

---

[4]Some hotels do have special check-in and check-out options for frequent guests or those who pay more for their accommodations.

to live in Sodom and he rose to prominence and popularity within the community. Lot gained vast riches and fame. He was thought of highly and esteemed by the worldly people in the town. When the Lord decided to destroy Sodom, Lot tried to warn his future sons-in-law, but his pleas fell on deaf ears. Lot's earlier tolerance of the lifestyles and immorality in Sodom had made him ineffective when he later tried to provide godly guidance. Similarly, tolerance of prejudices in ourselves and others today can have the same effect on our ability as Christians to witness and represent Christ. Here are just a few ways in which unchecked prejudices can be detrimental, especially in the lives of Christians.

Prejudices can limit our exposure. Most of us are more comfortable around people we know. That's to be expected. As Christians, most of our friends are Christians. This means that we spend the majority of our time around other Christians. But one of our main goals as Christians is to reach out to the unsaved and tell them about Jesus. The majority of the *work of the church* begins when we leave the sanctuary (as opposed to "church work," which I define as activities that generally occur within the church walls). The Great Commission instructs us to go and teach all nations, baptizing them in the name of the Father, Son and Holy Spirit (Mt 28:19-20). This challenge has no limits—no racial, sexual, cultural, ethnic, political or social boundaries. The phrase "all nations" includes everyone. Limiting ourselves to certain groups of people means only partially following the Great Commission. Jesus spent his life doing good for others and in death doing the ultimate good for all. Christ often interacted with diverse groups—the outcasts, the poor, the maimed and sinners. Although it did not exist as we know it during his lifetime, for Christ, living the principles of the Great Commission meant associating with people very unlike himself.

Prejudices can render us unable to appreciate the differences in others. A writer once said that diversity is the spice of life. I was in San Francisco on business several years ago. While sightseeing I immediately noticed the many diverse groups living and interacting together. White men were talking with African American men, Asian women were with white women, and African American women were interacting with Hispanic men. Although I was not privy to the extent of these relationships, what I saw gave me hope and inspiration. I'm sure you're thinking, *No big deal. That happens all the time where I live.* Yes, this also takes place in the city where I used to live. What impressed me most was the interaction between such a large number of diverse people. When we establish relationships and friendships with people from other races, cultures, social groups and backgrounds, we truly learn about diversity and how to better appreciate it. But prejudice results in the opposite: where differences in others are considered unattractive, foreign, inferior and often fearsome.

Prejudices can cause missed opportunities to witness. I was once asked to speak at a Christian women's retreat. As I prepared my session, I was intentional about including Scripture and scenarios that would both encourage and challenge participants. The session was received extremely well—my presentation seemed to be what was needed, and I was pleased to be able to share with the participants. However, another one of the speakers was not pleased. Although she initially appeared friendly, her later comments were indicative of intrasex prejudice based on credentials and education. During her presentation (that followed mine), she commented somewhat sarcastically that, although she was not an "educated, eloquent" speaker, she believed that the retreat should not focus on how-to sessions and structured presentations—God was calling Christian women to something else. She went on to say that she was not going to speak on her assigned topic. Instead, she led the women in a short activity, ended her session and abruptly left soon after. Her comments were sharp, pointed and tinged with anger. I got her message loud and clear. I (and other participants) felt that this speaker's comments grew out of preconceived notions about me based on educational attainment and perceived status (some attendees referred to me as "Rev. Dr." and my biographical summary in the program listed my educational and writing history). The speaker *assumed* that, because I was a college professor and writer *and* because my session was structured like a teaching/learning experience (I'm a teacher, that's what I do), I would somehow look down on her and what she had prepared—and that I somehow thought I was better. She had prejudged me and responded in a negative fashion.

What concerned me most was that she allowed her prejudices against me to prevent her from fully witnessing to and sharing with all the retreat participants (I noticed that she had some written information, but chose not to share it). I believe the retreat group would have welcomed her contribution—I know I would have—but the opportunity was missed. It was also disheartening to experience prejudice at the hands of another woman—during a retreat focused on empowering Christian women!

Many opportunities to witness present themselves at the most unexpected times, with and through the most unexpected people. Prejudices can influence whether and how we witness. Unchecked prejudices can bring about needless mistrust, negative feelings, or lack of godly love and cause us to avoid witnessing to others. We may not even be aware that our prejudices have affected our witnessing and believe that we are doing all that God requires of us. However, the consequences can be long-term, life changing, and detrimental to our ministries and personal testimonies.

Prejudices can enable Satan (and society) to use us. Satan will use every chance he can get to misdirect and mislead. Remember, prejudices and discrimination can undermine God's desire to reconcile humanity back to God. Yet this is what Satan desires to meet his objectives. Satan will try to influence what we say, think and do. We may have the false assumption that since Satan is not motivating us to act out some diabolical way, he is not influencing us. The truth is, Satan may also try to keep us inactive regarding something God wishes us to say or do. Sins of omission are just as displeasing to God as sins of commission. When we see situations around us that are not pleasing to God and we fail to get involved to stop them, we are accepting this behavior and silently condoning it. We are challenged to realize how God wishes us to respond in a given situation. Think back. Do you remember saying, doing or thinking something unkind and being convicted that what you had done was wrong? I can. What does this have to do with prejudices, you might ask? Satan can use our prejudices to hurt others and ourselves. During slavery in America, slaves were told to obey their masters no matter what. Scriptures such as Colossians 3:22 and Ephesians 6:5 were used to try to keep slaves under control. Satan as well as societal and personal desires for wealth motivated slave holders to use racial prejudices to not only physically enslave a nation of people of African descent, but to also spiritually, mentally and emotionally enslave all those involved—and to use the Bible to support it.

Prejudices can cause missed blessings. Because of prejudices, many Christians miss blessings in the form of friendships, more effective ministry and exposure to the diverse lives of others. I often wonder how many single persons have allowed their prejudices (based on weight, size, race, type of job, skin color, physical imparities, ethnicity, facial features or class) to prevent them from "seeing" the mate God has chosen for them. For example, studies show most women consider gainful employment to be the primary criteria for a "marriageable male" (W. Wilson 1996) and may consciously or unconsciously exclude potential spouses who possess character and other traits needed to sustain a relationship, but who don't earn a lot of money. When this occurs, it is an example of missed blessings due to class-based prejudices. In other cases, we miss blessings when we are unable to embrace diversity. For example, some churches choose to relocate when minorities begin to move into the neighborhoods in which they reside (McRoberts 2003). I often wonder what blessings for ministry are lost when this happens. Just think of the many other blessings that are within our grasp if we would always heed God's command: a stronger Christian testimony, more sisterly and brotherly love, material possessions and added spiritual strength, just to name a few. By no means am I suggesting a "give to get" mentality where we do God's will in the hope of receiving blessings. This point merely reminds us of the harmful spiritual and practical limitations of prejudices.

READ ABOUT

- **Christians and Fear:** 2 Timothy 1:7; Psalms 27

FOR PEACE

O Lord my God, in you I take refuge;
save me from all my pursuers, and deliver me.

Psalm 7:1

Interacting with people can be a challenge. Each person brings his or her own set of experiences to an encounter. Our "baggage" can result in negative or positive actions and reactions. Victims of prejudice have had to deal with the negative baggage of others. These prejudicial experiences, in turn, may have caused them to act and react in certain ways and may have also resulted in negative emotions. Some of these negative feelings include anger, denial, depression, self-doubt and self-hate, and fear.

Anger

Why do they treat me this way? Why won't they give me a chance? The harder I try, the more prejudice I face. At work, at school, in my neighborhood, at restaurants—even the kid at the check-out counter at the supermarket treats me as if he's *doing* me *a favor by ringing up my groceries! Can I ever find peace? Who do* they *think they are anyway? Will this ever end? It's the twenty-first century—and sometimes I think things are worse than they were when I was young. It scares me to think about what my children might have to face. Sometimes I get so mad . . . I could just explode!*

People who face prejudices may feel this way. They may feel a sense of disbelief and futility that results in anger. Some may feel trapped in a situation that is beyond their control. Others wonder what is wrong with those who are prejudiced—and reduce them to evil and inhumane objects. Prejudice is illogical. It just doesn't make sense. But when it is experienced, most people try to understand or analyze it. When this is not possible, many internalize their pain and anger. Some lash out at those who caused the pain. Others lash out at their loved ones or other innocent persons. Some may walk around carrying a chip on their shoulders—daring anyone to knock it off. West's (1993) examination of some of the results of urban poverty illustrates this point. While liberals and conservatives argue amongst themselves about the causes of social problems among severely impoverished inner city residents and provide Band-Aid solutions, West contends that neither camp is dealing with the *nihilistic* threat: the meaninglessness, hopelessness and lovelessness often felt by such persons. According to West, extreme poverty, discrimination and a life largely segregated from society means that growing numbers of the poor, especially young African Americans males, are being consumed by chaos and angst that affects them economically, socially, politically and spiritually. For West, U.S. flaws associated with prejudices, inequality and stereotypes result in considering poor African Americans the *problem* rather than as American citizens *with problems*.

West suggests that for the day-to-day lives of many such persons, moments of experiencing poverty and prejudices and their side-effects become hours, hours become days, days become weeks, weeks become months, months become years, and years become a lifetime. It's more than some people can handle. Sometimes people break under the strain. Logical ways to handle conflict seem ineffective; they've tried them time after time with little or no success. Some may feel that the time for rational discussion is over, the time for action is long overdue. The beliefs and behavior of Malcolm X during his early years and those of some members of the Black Power Movement reflect the negative results of continual exposure to prejudices (Morris 1984; Haley 1973). Many members of society are shocked by fights, riots and other negative confrontations that take place as a response to prejudice. Some wonder, why can't they just talk things over calmly and rationally—or demonstrate or boycott civilly? Just as prejudice is illogical and can cause devastating emotional, psychological and physical toil, unchecked anger by those who experience prejudices can also result in illogical, irrational and devastating events.

Denial

Denial can prevent us from admitting our own shortcomings and cause us to blame others for our troubles. Jimmy lived in a trailer park in south Georgia. Neither he nor his wife graduated from high school and his family was quite poor. They worked hard, but they could not afford to take care of their three children. It seemed as if the harder they worked, the poorer they got. Jimmy had been called "poor white trash" all his life, and although he had a tough guy image, he secretly envied those who had nice cars, expensive clothes and spending money. One day Jimmy decided to get some money. Why should he continue to suffer while others lived in luxury? He and a friend decided to rob a store. They were caught and arrested. Jimmy quickly blamed "the system" that continues to help the rich at the expense of the poor. He blamed society for keeping him down. The upper classes always have an advantage over the lower classes, he screamed.

Mobility studies do show that, in fact, middle and upper class people have a better chance of "moving up" in the world than poor people

(Blau and O. Duncan 1966; G. Duncan, Boisjoly and Smeeding 1996; O. Duncan 1979). Research also shows that minorities and the poor (regardless of the latter's race or ethnicity) tend to get longer jail sentences than whites and people from wealthy families who commit the same crime, respectively.[5] Yes, there are many inequities in society that should not be ignored or minimized. But what about Jimmy? What level of personal responsibility should he take for his criminal act? Did his impoverished existence justify attempted robbery? Was this his only option? Although Jimmy faced many obstacles because of his economic condition, this did not justify his negative behavior. Addressing prejudices requires collective and individual evaluation and change. This also means continually examining ourselves objectively for shortcomings and continuing to do our best despite obstacles.

Depression

I can't take it any longer. I've had enough. When prejudices become too much for some people to bear, instead of reacting angrily, they may become depressed. Instead of lashing out, they retreat. Such persons internalize their pain until it makes them ill. Here are a few examples. After years of rejection because she does not meet the "ideal" feminine image, Joan has given up on ever having a relationship. Although Curtis earned a college degree, found a good job and is now a productive member of society, he knows he will never be fully accepted or respected because of his skin color. Donna is a single mother. She is tired of being looked down upon, considered "loose" by men or just another statistic used to show that the American family is falling apart. Persons who experience prejudices may become so depressed that they simply give up. These persons may lose hope that things will get better (West 1993). Some may turn to temporary forms of relief such as medication, drugs or alcohol. They don't believe they have the strength to handle another day of ill treatment and disparaging attitudes. They've been beaten down by prejudices and peace is nowhere to be found.

---

[5]On disparities in incarceration rates based on race and forms of inequality, see Sorenson, Hope and Stemen 2003; Brownsberger 2000; Arvanites and Asher 1998.

Self-Doubt and Self-Hate

Maybe what they say about us is true. Maybe we are inferior. Maybe they are right, maybe as a woman, I am too aggressive. What kind of man am I? I can't even earn enough to take care of my wife and family! I thought I got the job because of my credentials, but maybe I was hired just to fill a quota.

When we begin to buy into prejudices, self-doubt often results. Instead of realizing that persons who hold prejudices are responsible for their negative views and/or behavior, we may wonder about our own self-worth. We wonder whether we fail to be accepted because we are somehow lacking. Self-doubt and insecurities affect how we view ourselves, our productivity and our relationships with others. Unchecked self-doubt can become self-hate. The noted theologian Dr. Cornel West wrote about reasons some African Americans may devalue themselves (1993). His observations suggest that society presents an ideal image of how persons should think, behave and look—and that this image is based on white standards. Persons who fit the standard are more likely to be accepted; those who do not are more likely to be rejected. If African Americans accept such images and fail to recognize the value found in themselves, some will begin to hate and devalue themselves because they deviate from the supposed ideal. West further argues that some persons may consider themselves inferior and begin to hate their differences: their intellect, lifestyles, noses, hips, hair and lips. This type of self-hate can ultimately result in persons who reject their culture, history, bodies and heritage. These observations can be applied to persons and groups other than African Americans. When prejudices cause persons to doubt and hate themselves, the effects are often long-term, devastating and difficult to overcome.

Fear

Fear is another emotion that often accompanies anger, denial, self-doubt and self-hate. Because of the long-reaching negative implications of this factor, I believe it is worthy of detailed review. Let's look at some of the possible fears of persons who often experience prejudices as well as how fears can affect their Christian testimony. Fear is often an illusive specter lurking in the shadows, far enough away that persons have some small sense of security, yet close enough to cause anxiety. Identifying and conquering fear is a popular subject. Given the myriad of articles, seminars, workshops, symposiums and self-help books on the subject, it would seem like we should be a fearless nation. In actuality, our fears appear to still get the best of us. What about persons on the receiving end of prejudices? What are some of the things they fear? What are they afraid of? Are there special anxieties and inner turmoil specific to experiencing prejudice? If they are Christians, how does this type of fear affect their testimonies? Let's examine some of the possible dimensions of fear for persons who experience prejudices.

Fear of rejection. Most of us are fearful of rejection—in friendships, relationships, even initial encounters. The fear of rejection seems timeless. In the Song of Solomon 1:1-6, the virgin feared rejection because of her dark, sunburned skin. Samson revealed the source of his strength out of fear of rejection by the relentless Delilah. Political candidates fear rejection by voters. Teenagers fear rejection by their first love (even Rudolph feared rejection because of his red nose). Why is rejection feared? Because most people take rejection personally, it can result in profoundly negative feelings. When rejection is based on prejudices, we may wonder, "Maybe they're right. Maybe their reasons for rejecting me have some merit." Feelings of insecurity and inferiority can creep in. Some people may even attempt to change themselves to please those that reject them. This type of peer pressure can cause great emotional turmoil.

An associate from Mexico commented on this dynamic. Paula came to this country with several friends. She was quite lonely, since most of her family was still in Mexico. Although she had found gainful employment and had acclimated fairly well, Paula had decided to return to her country. She enjoyed living in America, but didn't like what she believed she had to give up to be accepted. Her friends who had come to the United States with her had given up most of their Mexican customs and traditions. They considered the "American" lifestyle superior to their own. According to Paula, they had become too Americanized. Paula didn't understand why she had to become like everyone else just to be accepted.

Rejection is an unpleasant experience. Paula's concerns about being rejected were linked to the process referred to as *assimilation. In her case, she was being directly and indirectly encouraged to fit in by adopting cultural markers found in the United States. Usually this involves changing the way one dresses and one's language, values and traditions. It is common to believe that diverse groups actually integrate into society, that is, adopt certain cultural patterns from the *majority group[6] but maintain those crucial to their own. But studies show that there are often perks and penalties associated with the degree to which minority groups *assimilate into the dominate culture (Mohl and Betten 1986; Zangwill 1921). Although the process of assimilation is typically associated with racial and ethnic groups, it can be applied to most minority groups. For example, single persons may fear rejection from the married majority and seek to assimilate by getting married to an unacceptable partner. Females in a majority-male workplace may be encouraged to assimilate by dressing in attire considered more traditionally masculine or taking on traits considered more masculine for fear of rejection or fear of being passed over for promotions or placed on the "mommy track." And white immigrants may change their names to more Americanized ones in order to fit into a society that tends to place more social value on people of European descent. However, because we fear rejection, it is often easier to blame ourselves than to realize that a decision to reject is actually made by the other person(s) involved in the interaction.

Fear of physical harm. "I'm going to beat you up!" Marilyn spit these words at me during third period class. She didn't like the way I dressed, how I combed my hair or how our sixth grade teacher Ms. Kites constantly seemed to praise my work. After school Marilyn was going to make me sorry for being the teacher's pet. *Four hours, . . . in four hours I was going to get beaten up!* I'd never been in a fight before. Oh, sure, I'd wrestled and tussled with my sisters, but I'd never been in a *real*

---

[6]Readers should note the use of the term "majority group" here focuses on persons of European descent (i.e., white persons) in the United States and refers to the varied privileges associated with *numeric* majority (literal numbers of people—over 70 percent of the U.S. population is white), the history of power and privilege had by whites in society as compared to nonwhites, and the tendency for persons in positions of great political, economic and social power in society to be white. Sociological studies suggest that these factors continue to foster a certain degree of "race privilege" for whites (especially white males), regardless of their economic, political or social position. Thus whites who lack wealth or do not control major institutions and organizations in society are still considered members of the majority group and are generally able to tap into its resources more than nonwhites.

fight. Someone could get hurt—and that someone was me! I couldn't stop my palms from sweating, my knees from shaking or my heart from racing. Have you ever been afraid of physical harm? Those who experience prejudices may face the very sobering reality of physical danger. It is becoming more common for people to violently act on prejudices. Newspapers, radio broadcasts and television newscasts report increased hostility in our society. Hate groups are growing in size and strength. Lynchings are a part of U.S. history, and some continue to mysteriously occur today.[7]

As recently as 1998, James Byrd, an African American male, was bound and dragged to his death in Jasper, Texas, simply because of his race.[8] This racially motivated case made national attention. Byrd was chained to the back of a truck and dragged about two miles. His head, neck and right arm were found about one mile from the rest of his mangled body. Three white males (John William King, Lawrence Russell Brewer and Shawn Allen Berry) with ties to the Ku Klux Klan were indicted for the brutal slaying. On June 7, 1999, one of these men was convicted and sentenced to death, while the other two still await trial. In another case in October of 2002, Roger McCann, a twenty-three-year-old African American man, was found mysteriously hanged to death in rural Indiana.

Gay bashing and gender abuse are also more commonplace.[9] The murder of Matthew Shepard in Wyoming in 1998 received national media attention and pointed to increased attacks on gays and lesbians (Rayburn, Earleywine and Davison 2003; Steinberg, Brooks and Remtulla 2003; Nolan, Akiyama and Berhanu 2002; Herek, Cogan and Gillis 2002; Green, Strolovitch, Wong and Bailey 2001). Reports of children bullying their peers who are somehow different have become more common as well.[10] Fear of physical harm only compounds the anxiety of those affected by prejudices. Is it safe to drive in certain areas? Live in certain parts of town? Send my children to certain schools? Although many members of society are appalled to learn of prejudicial encounters that

---

[7]D. Grant 1975; Hayes 2000; Quarles 1987. Also read about the crusade against black lynching by Ida Wells-Barnett 1969, 1970.

[8]Also refer to academic articles by Levin 2002 and Perry 2002.

[9]Rayburn, Earleywine and Davison (2003) on hate crimes linked to physical and sexual assault.

[10]For traditional academic studies on bullying, refer to Seals and Young 2003; Sjostrom 1996; Stones 1993. Webster-Doyle (1991) provides children-friendly presentations on the subject.

escalate into violence, they also appear to be reluctant or powerless to effectively address systemic factors from which such behavior stems.

Fear of impotence. Society praises and rewards those who take control. Promotions are given to those who can effectively take charge and make things happen. So-called movers and shakers are applauded as role models in business. We enjoy being around people who know how to get things done. Although we can't control everything that takes place around us, most people pride themselves on being in control of their lives. But we can't control prejudices in others. No matter how we try, we cannot change a person's attitudes or beliefs. Laws in place to punish violence and discrimination that result from prejudices serve as deterrents, but are faulty because they provide society with guidelines to respond only to the *consequences* of prejudices. They cannot erase a prejudicial experience once it has occurred. People must choose to change.

A series of riots took place in Ontario, Canada, following those in Los Angeles in 1992 in response to the Rodney King decision. The mayhem, destruction and violence was the central topic of discussion in the media. I had been in Canada on business and was on a return flight. The chaos of the preceding weeks had taken its toll on me; I was sad, disillusioned and physically exhausted. A nap on the flight would do me good. As I reclined in my seat, I couldn't help but overhear the vocal conversation between two white women seated in the row behind me. The discussion was quite one-sided; the older woman seemed to be doing most of the talking. She spoke of her disgust at "all" the minorities who were part of the riots in Ontario. Instead of getting jobs, she said, they just looted and stole from others. Her blanket statements included phrases like, "trouble makers," "those people" and "hot-tempered." At first, I was simply going to ignore her remarks, but as she continued, I felt the need to address her stereotypes and sweeping generalities. I turned around in my seat and stated that I agreed with her that the riots were terrible, but that all minorities had not taken part in them or condoned such behavior. I further stated that her general statements were unfair to those who weren't involved and failed to consider the attitudes and behavior of nonminorities who had also been involved in the rioting. She initially seemed stunned by my remarks, but only commented to her friend, "See, I told you so." The experience seemed pointless—I had wasted my breath. Despite my statements, I was powerless to change the woman's views. I felt a sense of impotence and futility.

Some persons who experience prejudice express feelings of impotence in a more violent way. For this group, facing a continual barrage of prejudices can finally take its toll. Having unsuccessfully tried to reconcile or compromise with bearers of prejudices, some recipients may decide to opt out of the whole mess. They give up. The kaleidoscope of negative emotions related to prejudices—anger, inner turmoil, fear, rage, sadness, confusion—may become too much to handle. Some people may explode, taking their frustrations out on the closest or first member of "that group" they meet—or even among each other. Many riots among the poor have been a result of unchecked feelings of impotence.[11]

Fear of being "the only." Life often seems easier if we have something in common with those around us. People say they want to be different, but walking to the beat of a different drummer may also result in prejudices. Some people have been able to parlay their differences into success—consider the many atypical television personalities. But many people seem to relish being as much like everyone else as possible (I call it the middle American syndrome). The attempt by some families to keep up with the elusive Joneses is but one example. Part of the reason why stems from the sense of security, connectedness and comfort associated with being in the majority—and the sense of insecurity often associated with being in the minority. Interestingly, studies suggest that low representation by minority groups who live in predominately white areas is generally not considered a problem for majority group members. For example, when there are only a few racial or ethnic minority families in a neighborhood, their white neighbors aren't usually concerned. However, as the number of minorities increases or becomes more visible, majority members may experience "group threat" and begin to think and behave in prejudicial ways toward the minority group. Put another way, when you are "the only" (for example, the only woman in a given department), you are generally not considered a threat to those around you and may be treated civilly.[12] However, this does not mean that you

[11]Note that the latter statement is not an excuse for such behavior, but rather a partial explanation for it.

[12]See Fossett and Kiecolt 1989; Kane 2003; Kunovich 2004 on the subject of group threat.

will not experience isolation, may be ignored or feel as if you are living or working in a fish bowl.

Being "the only" can also result in increased anxiety. I once visited a small rural town in central Mexico. It was a beautiful, picturesque locale in the mountains, known for its handmade pottery and authentic Mexican food. I was excited about the trip, but I was not prepared for the reception. Based on the reactions and responses from most of the townspersons, you would have thought I was a ghost. People stared, children pointed, older people sneered, people in cars rubber-necked as they passed. It was very disconcerting and uncomfortable. I was later told by our host that most of the town's residents had never seen an African American in person, and my dark skin was all the more atypical. I questioned why—if they had never actually met an African American—so many persons were openly rude. She stated that the few television images they know about African Americans portray us as persons in abject poverty or involved in illegal activities. Thus many of the townspeople were having difficulty reconciling their initial exposure to an African American with the negative images they had been *socialized to believe. And because I was "the only" I bore the brunt of their negative stares and comments. If being "the only" in the past has resulted in prejudice, you may be all the more reluctant to be placed in a similar situation. If those around you harbor prejudices because you stand out, you may become the target of criticism and poor treatment. And even more troubling, if this happens, as "the only," who do you go to for redress?

Fear of the truth. The truth hurts. Persons who are prejudiced often have difficulty facing the truth when they have prejudicial attitudes or when they discriminate. By the same token, some persons who deal with prejudices may have difficulty facing certain truths. My friend Bruce had dealt with prejudices all his life. He often told me about negative experiences at the hands of Southern police officers. These encounters had left Bruce emotionally scarred and defensive. Once, while I was out driving with Bruce he was stopped by a police officer for breaking the law. Bruce mused silently, *But I was only driving 80 in a 60 mile-an-hour zone—everyone does it!* He became irate with the officer and accused him of mistreating him because he was a minority. Although he was clearly in the wrong, Bruce blamed the officer. However, Bruce had not been cited because he was a minority but because he had broken the law. His race or ethnic background was not the reason. But no amount of discussion could make Bruce believe otherwise. Sometimes we fear the truth because it may reveal things about us we don't want to admit. It was easier for Bruce to blame the officer for the traffic ticket than to admit that he had been irresponsible. The truth is no respecter of persons. If we accept it, the truth may reveal areas of needed improvement in our lives or character flaws. Admitting the truth may mean admitting that there are things about us that need to change. Just as it is foolish to believe that prejudices do not exist in our society, it is equally foolish to attribute every negative experience to prejudices.

Fear of showing frailties. We all pride ourselves on our ability to deal with life's challenges. It is important to exhibit self-efficacy—to be able to take care of oneself. No one wants to admit that a situation or series of experiences has become more than he or she can handle. In a society where power is usually rewarded, we learn to avoid situations and circumstances that are disempowering or that make us feel powerless. For example, some studies show that persons who face extreme poverty take pride in their ability to sustain their families and often blame *themselves* for the impoverished conditions around them. And although the choices individuals make influence their experiences in life, a large body of literature points to *structural forces such as globalization, deindustrialization and historic discriminatory practices rather than individual initiative as the primary reasons for much of the poverty in the United States.[13] A similar desire for self-efficacy can occur among those who face prejudices.

"Oh, I can handle it" or " I'm tough enough to deal with it" may be excuses to mask mountains of emotional scarring and psychological baggage. When faced with prejudices, it is important to admit hurt, pain or frustration. If these types of negative emotions go unchecked, they can fester and result in bitterness. When we become bitter, the bearer of prejudices has won, for the recipient continues to bear the pain of the experience long after the actual episode. However, some writers argue

---

[13]Refer to Katherine Newman (1999) *No Shame in My Game: The Working Poor in the Inner City* and Jay MacLeod (1995) *Ain't No Makin' It*.

that we live in a culture of victimization where people are reluctant to take personal responsibility for their actions and seek to blame others for their misfortunes. According to these writers, belief in *rugged individualism (that each of us is largely responsible for his/her own destiny) is dwindling and the ranks of the victimized now even include groups that have not experienced historic, long-term discrimination (e.g., claims of reverse racism among middle-class, white college students and white males in employment settings).[14] If our society is becoming more rights oriented such that persons who actually face prejudice and seek redress are considered recipients of special treatment, it may make it more difficult to accurately and objectively identify those involved in prejudicial situations (bearers and recipients). Furthermore, persons who actually experience prejudice may be less willing to admit their experiences and may be less likely to be believed by others.

Fear of the unknown. *Will my next experience be like the last one? Should I expect similar treatment? I'll hope for the best and prepare for the worst.* These are the types of questions and concerns that can plague persons who have experienced prejudices. New experiences are often not viewed with anticipation but with trepidation. Meeting new people can become anxiety-ridden experiences as one's mind becomes riddled with the fear of a repeat performance. You keep your guard up. In response, such persons may attempt to control or limit their exposure to situations that may prove hurtful. This protective mechanism works, but it can also be personally stifling and emotionally draining. It can also lead to social isolation. Studies on social isolation suggest that people who close themselves off (or are systematically closed off) are usually at a disadvantage. By limiting interaction to a narrow group of family and friends or remaining in a finite residential area, such persons are unable to develop the types of relationships or have access to important information needed to better themselves. These types of studies tend to focus on lost resources such as information about jobs, limited networks and subsequent economic problems.[15] However, it is also important to consider the emo-

---

[14]See Etzioni 1991 and Taylor 1991 on the culture of victimization.

[15]See Granovetter (1973, 1993) and Massey and Denton (1993) for examples of how limited informal ties and undue reliance on close familial relationships and isolation in urban settings are linked to economic problems.

tional and psychological disadvantages of isolating oneself—especially as a result of fears about prejudices. Persons who harbor prejudices may isolate themselves socially from groups they devalue or disparage; persons who experience prejudices may isolate themselves to avoid being devalued or disparaged. In both instances, fear of unknown situations and people undermine the ability to counterattack vestiges of previous negative experiences and to possibly develop healthy interactions.

Results of Fear

Some studies show that certain types of fear can be beneficial. For example, fear may enable persons to recognize and avoid danger or fear of reprisal may cause persons to avoid behavior that is illegal or unhealthy. However, these examples do not reflect fear that can be debilitating and do not parallel the types of fear I am focusing on here. Based on the types of fear outlined in this section, most people would agree: fear is not our friend. Fear can be especially stifling in the life of a Christian. It limits our power and robs us of peace. This type of fear is not of God. In 2 Timothy 1:7 we are reminded, "For God hath not given us the spirit of fear; but of power and of love, and of a sound mind" (KJV). How and why can fear resulting from prejudices be so devastating—especially for Christians?

Fear can limit our exposure. Jamie had had a difficult childhood. He had not done well in school, had fallen in with the "wrong" crowd and ended up in jail for robbery at the age of seventeen. After his release five years later, Jamie discovered that his incarceration experience made it almost impossible for him to find employment and get back on track. Jamie's mother had come to the church for assistance with her son. Brother Peterson—an active church member, leader of several ministries and male role model—was asked to mentor Jamie. However, the charge to work with Jamie was a new challenge for Brother Peterson. Jamie's time in prison had made him suspicious, bitter and angry. He was eager and "street-smart" but lacking in social skills. Although people at the church were glad he was out of prison, Jamie made some of them feel uncomfortable, even afraid—Brother Peterson included! Although Brother Peterson spoke to Jamie when they saw each other at church and encouraged Jamie not to give up, that was the extent of their interaction. He had been asked to establish a relationship with Jamie (and the young man wanted and sorely needed it), but Brother Peterson made excuses about why he could not spend time with Jamie and why his time would be better spent with boys with a better chance of "making it" in life. Brother Peterson was genuinely afraid of Jamie. Media representations and stereotypes about the "angry black male," concerns about high recidivism rates for the previously incarcerated and fear about potential danger from Jamie made Brother Peterson afraid. And his fear prevented him from providing the mentoring the young man truly needed. As time passed, Jamie's mother no longer asked Brother Peterson to intervene. Jamie eventually left the church and the city.

Like Brother Peterson, prejudices can make us leery of involvement with certain people or groups. However, Christians are challenged by the Great Commission to proclaim God's Word and live the example set forth by Jesus Christ. When we give in to fear resulting from prejudices, we are less effective, and we hold back from going that extra mile.

Fear can overshadow our spiritual gifts. Although prejudice is often associated with whites versus blacks, it is important to remember that other types of prejudices also exist. It is also important to remember that persons who experience prejudices can harbor them as well. After being on the receiving end of prejudices, it can become easier to say, "All those people think or act like that," and it may become easier to build up emotional walls and group others in stereotypical categories based on our negative experiences. A colleague, Andrew, relocated to a university town to take a job as a professor. Upon arriving, "town versus gown" dynamics were evident. Although most people seemed to get along, there were divisions, both perceived and real, between some local residents and university faculty. These divisions were also apparent in some congregations. Andrew was told which churches were frequented by the professors, which were frequented by working-class residents, which were more charismatic and which were more reserved. He was also discouraged from interacting with the locals, but refused to embrace such classism and elitism. After joining a church where the majority of members were local residents, Andrew, a Christian and Sunday school teacher for many years, became a Sunday school teacher. He welcomed the opportunity to teach again and become actively involved in this new community. His joyful experiences were short lived.

Most of Andrew's problems at the church stemmed from two longstanding members. Brothers Smith and Jones had "known the Lord" all their lives and made it clear that they "knew the Word." They were well known and held high positions in the congregation. Furthermore, although not formally trained, they were suspicious of people who "had book sense, but no common sense." Both men had experienced classism[16] and other negative episodes at the hands of some professors from the university and now believed most professors were snooty, self-absorbed people with god-complexes. By default, they were leery of Andrew. They questioned his sincerity and motives, attempted to undermine his teaching and on several occasions voiced their dislike of him. Andrew's Sunday school class had grown tremendously and the majority of people welcomed his teaching. However, after several years of strained, increasingly negative interactions, Andrew grew disillusioned about "those uneducated town folks" and decided to move his membership. He now travels sixty miles to attend church in a nearby larger city.

In this example, Andrew experienced prejudice because of his education and class standing. Although it may seem more common to expect persons who are formally trained to harbor prejudices against the less educated (and this does occur), Andrew's experience reminds us that prejudice can take many forms. Andrew's experiences are also troubling because they occurred between Christians and, in this case, undermined God's ministry (Andrew's Sunday school class has lost a skilled, dedicated teacher, and Andrew has left a growing teaching ministry). When this occurs, prejudices claim a twofold victory—the bearers *still* harbor prejudices and now the recipient may harbor prejudices as well. And the vicious cycle continues—but with a new participant.

Fear can prevent a healthy sense of self. I enjoy watching home improvement shows on television. I am hooked on the shows where the hosts are able to redesign entire rooms for very little money. One show in particular is quite impressive because the design crew revamps a room usually for under $50 using things from the owner's home—amazing! However, I noted a pattern among homeowners. When they are

---

[16]Prejudice based on differences in economic status and other factors usually related to economic status or social class such as educational attainment and wealth.

asked the type of room they want to have, most request home décor that is French country or Tuscan, French provincial or Italian. Most homeowners want their homes to look like those found in other countries and cultures. I understand that such requests may simply reflect an appreciation of diversity, but I wonder whether part of it is also due to the tendency to esteem others more than ourselves ("the grass is always greener" mentality). Few homeowners request renovations that reflect U.S. motifs and styles.

Similarly, exposure to prejudices may result in an unhealthy sense of self—where persons esteem other groups and cultures more than themselves and their own and devalue what they have to offer (i.e., their aptitude, physical features, skills and gifts). I know an African American college professor who is extremely knowledgeable about many different racial and ethnic groups and their cultures. He has performed extensive research on their lifestyles, customs and histories. He can talk for hours about these groups and always praises them. However, he seems to know very little about African Americans and African American culture. Others groups seem to be superior in his estimation. His views manifest themselves in overcritical comments and stereotypes about African Americans, avoidance of them and descriptions of himself that minimize his African American heritage. Because he was raised in the 1950s South and experienced a great deal of discrimination, I believe these experiences have resulted in internalized negative feelings about his race, ethnicity and heritage. Just as prejudices can reflect an unhealthy, inflated, overly positive sense of self for bearers, it can also make it difficult for recipients to view themselves favorably.

Fear can cause missed opportunities to witness. Donna was part of a ministry with an inner-city housing project. She was responsible for providing counseling to women recently released from prison. This required her to travel into many different types of neighborhoods—sometimes into high crime areas. On this particular day, she had promised a woman she'd visit her and Donna did not want to go back on her word. Donna had become particularly attached to the young woman, who was working valiantly to find a job and make a new life. Donna hoped that her encouragement and practical aid would help the young woman make a smooth transition back into the workforce. The woman lived in a high crime area and Donna felt uneasy about visiting her alone, but she remembered her promise and went. After their visit ended, Donna was about to go to her car, but a group of men near her car caused her to halt. What should she do? Donna was afraid. Maybe she shouldn't have come. Maybe her initial concerns were founded.

As Donna walked toward her car, the woman she had just visited came out of her apartment. Together they walked toward Donna's car. The young woman spoke to the men. They returned her greeting and also spoke to Donna. The men turned and continued to talk among themselves. Donna never knew whether her fears about the men were founded, but she thanked the young lady anyway. The young lady replied, "You've been so helpful to me, I couldn't pass up a chance to help you." Donna did not allow her initial fears to prevent her from reaching out to a woman in need of love and support. She saw an opportunity to help and she made herself available. Not only did God protect Donna in her obedience, but provided an opportunity for the young woman to help Donna as well.

Fear can make one unable to appreciate diversity. My friend's son Stephen is the typical rambunctious, inquisitive six-year-old. He's always on the go and always into things. A person can get tired just *watching* him play. At home, Stephen can often be found in his underwear with a bath towel draped around his neck. He enjoys pretending to be a superhero—but he doesn't pretend to be Batman or Ironman, not even Superman. Stephen stops crime and "saves" his mother from danger as—"Strongerman!" I laughed when his mother told me about Stephen's nontraditional crime fighter. Stephen is a typical little boy, but his thoughts are often atypical. Just as Stephen imagined a different type of superhero, there are many different types of people (i.e., *intergroup differences). Different attitudes, beliefs and behavior can also be found among people of similar backgrounds (i.e., intragroup differences). All rich people do not think and act alike. All men do not think or act alike. Nor do all gays and lesbians—or all racial or ethnic groups. Fear can hinder our ability to understand and appreciate differences in others. When we isolate ourselves as protection from prejudices, we often miss out.

Sociologists often write about the implications of "gatekeeping." This phenomenon occurs when persons or groups are systematically prevented from access to information and resources by other persons and groups in power. Those who are "kept out of the gate" are at a disadvantage, and those who are "inside the gate" usually benefit from these exclusionary tactics. Gatekeeping applies here because prejudices that advance to discrimination can result in gatekeeping (for example, the glass ceiling for women and minorities in some corporate settings, redlining in poor urban neighborhoods or refusing to accept viable candidates for group membership because of race, skin color, sexual orientation or family history). Gatekeeping usually results in homogeneous groups, both inside and outside the "gate." This also means that many persons who have experienced prejudices have also been on the receiving end of gatekeeping. And just as persons who harbor prejudices may take part in gatekeeping, those who experience prejudices may put up gates or walls as a coping mechanism that prevents them from recognizing and appreciating diversity. Our society has been referred to as a melting pot. A better analogy suggests a tossed salad where varied groups mix and mingle together, but still retain those differences that make them unique. By placing barriers around themselves, persons who have been hurt because of their differences hinder their own ability to learn about and possibly appreciate differences in others.

Fear can cause missed blessings. Sociologist Thorstein Veblen (1953) coined the term "conspicuous consumption" to describe the practice of buying cars, homes, clothes and jewelry in order to prove something to other people. Such persons attempt to make a statement to others: "I am successful" or "I am wealthy" or "I am happy" or "I am fashionable" or maybe "I am better than you, and I have more *stuff* than you do." Conspicuous consumption often involves going overboard—flashy clothes, big cars and big homes—in an attempt to impress others and exhibit our abundance of earthly possessions (refer to T. Veblen 1953). But these things can't buy peace. Peace is a gift, a blessing from God. We all know or have heard about people who spend large sums of money or abuse their bodies and minds all with the hope of chasing away fears. But I don't know of anyone who has been successful. Fear squelches peace, but it also limits our spiritual productivity because God can't effectively use us for kingdom building. This also means that we are stymied from the spiritual growth that comes from being used by God. It limits our growth in character, resolve, faith, patience and love, just to name a few. Fear can also limit God's ability to physically bless us. When fear limits our blessings, it can also prevent us from being a blessing to others. Unlike a worldly focus on conspicuous consumption as a sign of earthly success, overcoming prejudice-related fears to the benefit of personal spiritual growth and ministry both serve as signs of spiritual success.

A Way to Overcome Fears

Someone may be thinking, *But how can I overcome my fears? How can I find peace? I've had negative experiences in the past and I'd rather not subject myself to that again.* It may be difficult to deal with fears related to prejudices. Past experiences can make it difficult to admit such fears, overcome them or trust those who have hurt us. Society often treats those who voice concerns as whiners or as losers who can't make it in the real world and make excuses and blame others for their state. But we must face negative emotions if God is to remove them. In her book *Soul Stories: African American Christian Education,* Dr. Anne Streaty Wimberly (1994) presents a process of story-linking that can be used to overcome fears. Although she focuses on African American experiences, her findings and observations are germane to addressing prejudices in general.

> Story-linking is a process whereby persons connect components of their everyday life stories with the Christian faith story found in Scripture. Participants also connect their personal stories with Christian faith heritage stories of African Americans outside Scripture. (p. 13)

According to Dr. Wimberly, by relating their own experiences with biblical and historical persons who have experienced victories over adversities, Christians become inspired and motivated and can overcome great odds, be liberated from oppressive attitudes and behavior, and become better prepared for ministry. Applying her strategies, persons can use biblical stories to address prejudices they face to find peace. Although I present a variety of other strategies to address prejudices for power and peace in chapter seven, story-linking provides one important avenue to reconcile negative experiences in general and those related to prejudices in particular. Wimberly continues:

> We assign meanings to the happenings in our lives and arrive at various degrees of understandings of our purposes, and we have a great deal to say about how our plots unfold. Indeed, we have a lot to say about whether our unfolding plots will be liberating or blocking for us and others. . . . When we become Christians, we choose a Christian story plot. . . . Our unfolding plot becomes defined by hope-filled purpose, based on God's ongoing *value of us* and expectation of *our valuing others*. (1994, p. 93, emphasis mine)

Using this approach, Scripture becomes a central mechanism to overcome prejudices for peace. Let's consider an example. In Matthew 11:28, Christ encourages us to "Come to me, all you that are weary and are carrying heavy burdens, and I will give you rest." Several words in this passage are key to ridding ourselves of prejudice-based fears.

"Come." Christ provides an open invitation. Because this word is a verb, it suggests action on our part. Yes, rest is available, but we have to *choose* to receive it. This means *asking* him to remove fears that limit our spiritual, emotional and psychological growth.

"Me." Only Christ can give rest. This means that we must have a relationship with the him. Christ is our link to the source from which healing comes. And as our Comforter, the Holy Spirit brings about renewal if periods of turmoil return.

"All." Everyone can receive rest. Whether we have experienced prejudices based on race, sex, color, age, ethnicity, sexual orientation, religion, physical appearance, creed or any other reason, peace is within our grasp. This word also suggests that although society seems to target certain groups, anyone can be a recipient of prejudices.

"Heavy burdens." Fears take their toll on us spiritually, emotionally and psychologically. Some may even have negative physical repercussions. Its weight may seem unbearable. In this passage, Christ acknowledges that we may become tired as a result of our experiences. We should note Christ is already aware of our fears; there is no need to be ashamed of or deny the fears that plague us. He is waiting for us to acknowledge them.

"Will." We all know the difference between the words *may, might, can, could*. These words suggest the possibility of some action or event. The word *will* indicates certainty. Christ promises us rest—no ifs, ands or buts about it.

READ ABOUT

- **Fear:** Luke 12:4-7
- **Worry:** Luke 12:22-34
- **Anger:** Ephesians 4:26-27
- **How Love Conquers Fear:** 1 John 4:18

"Rest." This is the goal. Rest can be defined as peace of mind or spirit. Jesus has promised us peace. It is within our reach. We don't have to buy it or barter for it. It is free. But we must first choose to accept Christ's offer if peace is to be attained.

Based on the story-linking process, Christians have peace at our disposal and scriptural steps available to attain it. The search for peace is also strengthened when biblical success stories are combined with stories of other people who have overcome prejudices for peace (for example, Martin Luther King Jr., Mother Theresa, a family member or friend). If you've faced prejudices in the past, you may face them in the future. There are no guarantees. Fear and other negative emotions may result. Christ did not promise that we wouldn't have such negative experiences. However, he did promise that through him, we could have victory over their effects.

4

An Effective Mentor

FOR POWER

You shall be holy, for I am holy.

1 PETER 1:16

So you realize that you harbor some prejudices—what then? How can they be eliminated? Can good intentions be converted into practical application? When change is needed, it is best to have a relationship with someone who can help make improvement possible. One suggestion is to find a mentor who can give you advice and support. Studies suggest that role models are largely the way people, especially the young, learn to become productive members of society. For example, research by William J. Wilson (1987, 1996) illustrates the importance of class-diverse urban communities. According to Wilson, poor and working class children growing up in cities like Chicago could see and interact with their neighbors who were doctors, teachers, lawyers and businesspersons. Thus, such persons were examples of what could be achieved through hard work, determination and education. Wilson's findings can be applied here to suggest that mentors or role models can help persons who are both trying to overcome prejudices for power and others who are seeking peace. Think of a mentor as a coach, someone who can be trusted to guide and teach.

Characteristics of a Mentor

A mentor is a role model whose lifestyle can be emulated. Some people have mentors who are famous or rich. But for Christians, the prerequisites for a mentor are different from those in society. The mentor we select should be someone whose Christian lifestyle is exemplary and, based on the topic in this book, someone who has faced but not succumbed to prejudices. Here are four characteristics to consider.

Someone who is a Christian. There are many non-Christians who are worthy of admiration and respect for their talents, character and contributions and who could make suitable mentors. However, because we are operating from a Christian perspective and our objective is to be Christlike, the *ideal* mentor should be someone who is saved and committed to Christ.[1] The Bible provides various good examples. David was considered a man after God's own heart (1 Sam 13:14); Job was described as perfect and upright (Job 1:1). Because of Solomon's selfless desire to lead God's people correctly; he was given wisdom, an understanding heart, riches and honor (1 Kings 3:7-14); Eunice and Lois were praised for their sincere faith (2 Tim 1:5); and few would challenge the unique place held by the apostle Paul as a writer, activist, leader, scholar and Christian martyr. Although imperfect, all these individuals can be considered examples of biblical role models.

Someone involved in your life. Close contact with you is a must. A mentor should have the desire and ability to be closely involved in your life to help you learn and grow. This interaction would go beyond just meeting periodically. The ideal mentor would be someone who knows you intimately and with whom you have a healthy, loving, positive relationship. This type of mentor would show you love that you, in turn, could show others.

Someone who has confronted prejudices. It can be very difficult to overcome prejudices. It requires self-reflection, admitting growth areas, changing the way you think, believe and behave, and understanding how society can influence you. (Note, for example, that Gaertner and Dovidio [1986] suggest that aversive racists may not even know they

---

[1]Persons who do not have access to Christian mentors (e.g., Christian students on secular campuses) should consider finding mentors among secular persons (e.g., select professors) they believe are of good character and who wish to provide them with guidance. However, it is important to remember the differences in the types of relationship that should be forged. A non-Christian can provide sound, helpful advice. However, she/he should not be expected to provide guidance based on biblical tenets. It is also important to remember that just because a person is a Christian does not automatically make him/her a suitable mentor.

are racists. Their findings provide one example of the ways in which prejudices can subtly exist.) This challenge can be more easily met if your mentor is someone who has successfully addressed prejudices because he or she has had experiences similar to yours and handled them appropriately. A good mentor should be able to calmly and directly confront and address prejudices. This type of mentor can help you understand your feelings and actions and make suggestions for positive change. And this person can be sympathetic because he or she knows what you are feeling. The very presence of such a person would be a motivator because he or she is an example of the ability to overcome prejudices.

Someone who motivates you to be your best. As a college professor, I am responsible for relaying a body of knowledge to students. My job requires me to give lectures, exams and projects, read assignments, hold office hours and prepare students to be their professional and personal best. Another responsibility students rarely remember (or appreciate) is my role to challenge them beyond their current ways of thinking and doing. This task assumes that students can be and do *more*—and that they will grow and improve when challenged beyond their present levels of understanding. Some students do not appreciate being challenged; they want to take classes that are easy A's. But A students are those who have done their very best in class—according to *my* classroom standard and not theirs. Similarly, a mentor would want you to follow the slogan "be all that you can be," and not to limit yourself. This person would encourage and motivate you to strive to maximize your potential and not settle for mediocrity. He or she would be available with advice as well as a helping hand—during good and bad times. When you needed an honest opinion, you could count on this person to tell the truth and admonish you when necessary. This type of mentor would not be a "yes person" who would simply tell you what you wanted to hear.

It may be difficult to find this type of mentor. We often need help to identify and acknowledge personal growth areas and then to actually change our attitudes or behavior. An effective mentor can provide objective suggestions, honest opinions, support, encouragement and constructive criticism. If you believe you have a possible candidate for a mentor, it may be helpful to also ask him or her the following types of questions: How have you addressed prejudices? Are you still working to overcome them? Which ones? How have you been successful up to this point? As the old saying goes, two heads are better than one. If you have someone to help you, working together to overcome prejudices may not seem as daunting.

Christ as the Ideal Mentor

It is important to remember that even the most Christlike role models are imperfect. They too are still maturing as Christians. They should have an important place in our lives, but earthly mentors cannot be idolized, for all have sinned and come short of God's glory. So while our earthly mentors should be godly people, they can never be God. "Well, is there a perfect mentor?" you might ask. Of course. Jesus Christ is the only perfect role model. He meets and surpasses all prerequisites. Let's compare the life and ministry of Christ to the characteristics of an effective mentor presented earlier.

Christ modeled the life of a perfect Christian. Hebrews 4:15 notes, "For we do not have a high priest who is unable to sympathize with our weaknesses, but we have one who in every respect has been tested as we are, yet without sin." John 1:14 further reminds us, "And the Word became flesh and lived among us, and we have seen his glory, the glory as of a father's only son, full of grace and truth." Not only was Jesus perfect in his heavenly state, but also remained so after taking human form. As a Jew living in a Jewish culture, Jesus cannot be characterized specifically as a "Christian" based on current definitions (the concept "Christian" as we understand it did not exist at that time). However, his life serves as the perfect model of Christian attitudes and behavior that we are challenged to emulate. He was able to live among women and men and be victorious over temptations to provide the perfect example for us. In *Kingdom Ethics: Following Jesus in Contemporary Context,* Stassen and Gushee (2003) focus on the life and teaching of Jesus Christ as the exemplar of Christian ethics. They contend that Christ's teachings, especially those presented in the Sermon on the Mount, can be applied when dealing with contemporary social issues such as racial differences and sexuality. Through their exegesis of his teachings, the authors show

how Christ valued all life, correlated love and justice and encouraged believers toward peaceful coexistence. Their work is germane here because they provide a convincing argument that Christ's words and deeds represent a real, practical set of guidelines that enable Christians to do the right thing.

Christ is involved in our lives. John 13:34; 15:12 and Romans 5:8 relay the depth and sincerity of Christ's feelings for humanity. His love was and is unconditional and unceasing. When we accept him as our Savior, he becomes more closely involved in our lives. Christ is always willing to deepen his level of intimacy with his followers; we determine the depth of this involvement. Christ loves us with an agape love and desires that we show this same type of love in our relationships with others (Okholm 1997; Evans 1995; Perkins and Rice 2000; Washington and Kehrein 1996). His encounters with the Samaritan woman (Jn 4:1-26), Zacchaeus the tax collector (Lk 19:1-10) and the woman with the issue of blood (Mt 9:20-22) are a few examples of how Christ showed us how to love, interact with and appreciate diverse people.

Christ confronted prejudices. Christ did not harbor prejudices, but he had to deal with people who misunderstood, devalued and feared him because he was different. He was confronted with prejudices. The biblical story of Jesus' response to the woman caught in adultery (Jn 8:1-11) provides an example of his response to prejudices. You may not have considered this story through the lens of prejudices, but in addition to being an example of forgiveness, the woman's predicament is an example of the double standard that existed (and still does today) regarding sexual behavior for males and females. Historically, female adultery was considered a transgression usually punishable by death.[2] However, males were not typically judged by the same standard (although if the adulterous act was heterosexual in nature, logically a male was involved).[3] When we consider the passage within the context of prejudices, the adulterous woman was about to be stoned because of sexist

---

[2]Female concubines were usually the exception to this rule.

[3]Although increasing numbers of married women are taking part in adultery, Wilson and Medora (1990) find that men are generally more likely than women to take part in extramarital sex. Buunk (1987) finds that husbands are less likely than wives to continue in a marriage after learning of a spouse's extramarital affair. Also Tanhill 1980.

views that condemned her behavior and tacitly ignored the behavior of her male partner. Jesus confronted the hypocritical crowd and challenged them to remember their own sins. He subsequently saved the woman both physically and spiritually. Scripture also reminds us that Christ was tempted just as we are, but he never sinned. This means that he understands what we face as we strive to conquer our prejudices. His model for living can provide instruction, encouragement and strength during the process.

Christ motivates us to be our best. In the Scripture "You shall be holy, for I am holy" (1 Pet 1:16), God challenges us to live a godly lifestyle. On our journey toward this goal, God is continually purging us in preparation for greater works. Motivation may take the form of blessings; sometimes chastisement is necessary. Our most valuable motivator is the life and legacy of Jesus Christ (Stassen and Gushee 2003). His continual tests by people and circumstances on earth inform our struggles to be victorious over prejudices. This type of motivation can fortify our resolve and enable us to act on what we have learned.

For example, it's common to seek heavenly guidance concerning milestones in our lives. Christians pray to God to confirm decisions about a potential spouse, an employment decision, a medical operation or a major financial purchase. Most of us seek God in these matters because we realize that these decisions can drastically affect our future. In some cases, the Lord's will is quite evident. In others situations, receiving direction from God involves fasting, prayer, pastoral consultations and personal Bible study. But most of us spend the needed time and energy because we know that the right decision is crucial. But is God's involvement in our day-to-day lives as evident? It may be difficult to view our daily experiences as the building blocks of our life's testimony, but they are. The majority of our lives are not spent making major decisions, but making a variety of small ones (for example, most people don't marry multiple times, change jobs or homes yearly or frequently make life and death decisions). But regardless of the perceived importance of a decision, spiritual guidance is important.

If you think about it, during the average day, you meet and interact with many people, Christians and non-Christians alike. Each encounter requires decisions in terms of how you feel about and treat those persons. Decisions made in haste without spiritual guidance may be contrary to God's will. If we are following Christ as our role model, it becomes unnecessary to stop and think about how to treat others. As we become more like Christ, it will become easier to view people as Christ did and to treat them as God would want. A personal example illustrates this point. One day it seemed as if I had twenty-six hours of things to do: attending church meetings, exercise class, grocery shopping, left-over work from my job, just to name a few. I did not know how I was going to get it all done, but I was determined to complete my "to do" list *that day*. One of my last stops was at a nearby grocery store. After scurrying through the lanes, dodging slower shoppers and unsuspecting children and tossing items haphazardly into the shopping cart, I finally arrived at the checkout counter. Quite a few teenagers were employed at the store—I'm guessing my check-out attendant was about sixteen years old. Since I shopped there often and knew many of the employee's faces, I also knew that he was a new hire.

As he began to ring up my items I noticed that he overcharged me for a product. I casually mentioned it to him and he, after confirming the price, input the correct amount. A few items later he keyed in another incorrect price. Again I pointed out his mistake, this time in a slightly more terse tone of voice. He realized his error, apologized and made the correction. Several items later, he again made the same mistake. As they say in baseball, three strikes and you're out. I had passed the point of understanding. In a restrained, yet forced tone of voice, I again made his mistake known to him. My words were few but very curt and dry—no need for many words—what I did not say verbally I screamed loudly with facial expressions. *Kids,* I thought. *He is much too young and inexperienced to have this job. I should not have to waste my time being the guinea pig for a trainee when I already have a million things to do!* (In retrospect, one could argue that my views were a form of ageism.) By this time, you can imagine how frazzled the young man was. He had lost all concentration, fumbled with the cash register and apologized profusely. After paying for my purchases I huffed out of the store, complaining to myself about the quality of service. I was steamed! As I drove home, I cooled off considerably (shame often causes the body temperature to drop several degrees). I thought about how I had treated that young store clerk. My grocery trip had been just one of many tasks to be done that day and the encounter with the clerk lasted about seven minutes. In other words, relative to the overall scope of my day, this was a small incident, but it had a big impact on me and probably on the young cashier. The problem was that I had left Christ and my desire to be like him out of that interaction.

Try to imagine Christ in my place in the checkout line. As the young clerk fumbled and stumbled while checking out his products, Jesus would have waited patiently. During his frequent mistakes and apologies, Christ would have said something reassuring like "We all make mistakes" or "You're new here? I know how hard it can be at a new job." Christ would have tried to make the young man feel better and more confident. Christ probably wouldn't have been concerned about being overcharged either. That was a test that I flunked with flying colors.

I would like to suggest an approach in dealing with day-to-day issues related to prejudice. During times when you find yourself at a crossroads, ask yourself, "What would Jesus do?" Although this is a common catch phrase today, it has important implications for daily interactions. Thinking about how Jesus handled certain situations will provide you with the insight to deal with them. Study Jesus' responses to people in the Bible. What did he say about the oppressed and downtrodden in the Beatitudes? How did Christ help his disciples understand the importance of children? Refer to his many parables that instruct us how we should interact with each other (the forgiving master, the unforgiving servant, the prodigal son).

Christ was different. He took time to understand people's experiences. He genuinely wanted to understand where they were coming from. He didn't focus on his own needs or rights, but on those of others. Christ did not fear rejection or being inconvenienced. And he experienced prejudices because of his differences. "Love your enemies. Do good to those who hate you." *Yeah, right . . . who is this guy?* were probably the sentiments of many who initially heard his message. Christ came with a new and different message and challenge—and he was rejected and ostracized by those who feared and misunderstood him and refused to get to know him. But their preconceived notions set in motion the chain of events that brought about salvation and the possibility for reconciliation. How was Christ able to live a prejudice-free life? How was he so easily able to appreciate human diversity? Christ was connected to God, the Power Source. His intimate relationship with God enabled him to embrace diversity. In John 10:30, he proclaimed, "the Father and I are one." This means that Christ had the power to reconcile all people to God and that the power came *directly from God.* We too, are connected to God, and we can think, believe and act as Christ did.

The description of God as the great I AM in Exodus 3:14 reflects a type of diversity. By God's very nature, the great I AM is able to understand, relate to, appreciate and genuinely love God's diverse creation. God is able to readily embrace us all—male, female, Native American, Asian, rich, poor, young or old. The threefold personality of the Trinity reflects diversity *and* commonality. Because of their nature, God, Jesus Christ and the Holy Spirit are able to exist as unique and common, separate and whole, three and one, simultaneously. I contend that this diversity enables the Trinity to appreciate the nuances found in creation. In addition, their commonalities enable them to bring reconciliation, both between God and humanity and between people. Our power lies in the ability to establish a relationship with this diverse Trinity (Deddo 1997). Christ's existence served as a living, breathing testimony of this diversity. He is the ideal mentor and most effective role model. If you remember, Christ's roster of friends, acquaintances, associates (and enemies) read like a *Who's Who of Diversity*—fishermen, Jews, children, cripples, prostitutes, doctors, the politically powerful, Gentiles, tax collectors, the poor, criminals, the wealthy, women with ailments, the demon-possessed, religious leaders and military leaders, just to name a few. No one was above or beneath his reach.

Some scholars point to Matthew 1:3-6 to suggest that Jesus' very genealogy reflected *interracial unions.[4] In addition, his teaching about the Good Samaritan and the Samaritan women, for example, instructed lis-

---

[4]Some scholars argue against this assessment because "race" as a social construct did not exist during Jesus' lifetime and suggest instead that Christ had a mixed "ethnic" genealogy. However, a similar counterclaim could be made about use of the term *ethnicity.* Rather than debate, readers are encouraged to refer to Keener's (1997) "The gospel and racial reconciliation" for his argument and supporting work.

teners toward love and acceptance. His actions when washing the disciples' feet showed love, humility, forgiveness and forbearance to be emulated. Scripture reminds us that God made humanity a little lower than the angels and that Jesus is our advocate who is not ashamed to call us brother (or sister) (Heb 2:7, 11-12). Because of what God did through Jesus Christ, as Deddo notes:

> All relationships are to bear witness to and thereby reflect God's own personalizing covenant love extended to us in Christ and by the Sprit. Those who contain their love for themselves and their own kind do not bear witness to the extensive love of God in Christ. The extension of our love to those who are different, even to enemies, is the test of the genuineness of our love. (1997, p. 61)

READ ABOUT

- **Who Christians Can Rely On:** Hebrews 4:14-16

Directly or indirectly, Christ touched the lives of humanity—past, present and future. Christ realized the importance of diversity, mutuality and the intrinsic value in others—so can we.

FOR PEACE

I have said this to you, so that in me you may have peace. In the world you face persecution. But take courage; I have conquered the world!

JOHN 16:33

I contend that the Peace Line, Jesus Christ, is the perfect mentor for reasons outlined earlier in this chapter. But his life experiences can also provide instruction for persons who experience prejudices. Were people ever prejudiced against Christ? Did they ever have preconceived notions regarding his lifestyle? How he should act? His purpose? If so, what did Jesus do? How did he react? Scripture suggests that Christ experienced prejudices at the hands of others. The Bible may not specifically identify certain experiences as prejudicial, yet Christ was often considered different, expected to act and think a certain way, and mistreated because of his lifestyle. Who were some of the people who harbored prejudices against Christ because he was different?

Religious Leaders

The Pharisees and the Sadducees misunderstood Christ and were quite elitist in their views about him. They were leery of him. Jesus said that he was the Messiah, and many people were beginning to believe him. Prior to Christ's arrival, the religious leaders held a very powerful and influential place in the lives of the people. Christ came and threatened to take all that away. To make matters worse, to them, he didn't even act like a religious leader, let alone a "king." Let's imagine some of the elitist conversations among these religious leaders: "This *Jesus* has been eating with sinners, seen with prostitutes and fellowshipping with tax collectors. What kind of Messiah is this? He appears to be nothing more than a self-made demagogue leading a group of fishermen who purposely mislead the people and dishonor the Sabbath. The fact that he heals the sick, feeds the poor and appears to care for the people is an obvious ploy to trick the masses and gain power. We are the genuine, rightful religious leaders, trained and credentialed to guide the people. He's sacrilegious—and he wants to take control!" The Pharisees and Sadducees didn't really know Christ, but they had made up their minds about him. His teachings and actions were mocked and devalued. Even when he did good deeds, Christ's intentions were suspect by others who believed they were better or more qualified leaders.

The Masses

The people anticipated a "deliverer," but many of them also had preexisting ideas and thoughts about what he'd be like. They predicted that he would look a certain way, think a certain way and act a certain way. Many believed that their king would overthrow the existing Roman government and save them from poverty and oppression. When Jesus did not meet their expectations, I can imagine some of their comments: "This *Jesus,* we've been following him for quite some time now. And although he gives us food, has great teaching lessons and heals people, he still hasn't taken his place as king. What's he waiting for? We're tired of living in ruin. We need a king who will lead us to victory. We'll fight, if necessary, but our king must tell us how, when and where. So far, all he talks about is love, peace and kindness. That's nice, but we're ready for the revolution—we're ready to take control!" The masses that followed

Christ daily were often unaware of his mission. Scripture notes that even the disciples were sometimes unclear about his true purpose. You may not have thought about Christ's earthly experience in this way. But it is helpful to realize that he faced many of the same types of prejudices and stereotypes we face today. And because he did, Christ provides the perfect role model for persons who experience prejudices. Let's examine some reasons why Christ was able to be victorious despite the preconceived notions and prejudices of others.

Jesus Knew Who He Was

His sense of self was intact. There was no need for confirmation or validation from the religious leaders or the masses. Skeptics were always present, but Christ continued to be himself. In the end, many came to realize who he was. Philippians 2:10-11 confirms that "at the name of Jesus every knee should bend . . . and every tongue should confess that Jesus Christ is Lord." Jesus knew this. Do you know who you are? Do you have a strong sense of self?[5] Most students who have taken an introductory sociology or psychology course have heard about Charles Cooley's (1964) concept, the "looking-glass self." According to Cooley, the image we have of ourselves is largely shaped by how we believe others perceive us. Using this thesis, if we believe others consider us unattractive, less intelligent or unworthy, we are more likely to accept and internalize these views. The broad textbook presentation of Cooley's concept suggests that people are largely social sponges who readily embrace the beliefs of others around them—even when those views are disparaging or inaccurate. However, a closer reading of Cooley's original work (*Human Nature and the Social Order,* 1964) illustrates that self-perceptions are developed through a dynamic process where people are influenced by the opinions of others, but also actively attempt to select and embrace those perceptions that are the most positive and flattering. Thus the looking glass through which we see "self" is influenced by whether and how we *choose* to accept the views of others. Is your sense

[5]Cooley 1964; Mead 1962; and Goffman 1959 have written extensively about the development of "self." However, as Christians, our spiritual sense of self is grounded in faith in the salvific act of Christ and God's love for us demonstrated when God allowed Jesus' sacrifice to take place.

of self and self-worth intact or do you often feel diminished because of prejudicial episodes? As was presented in chapter three, prejudices can result in insecurity and self-doubt. But understanding, appreciating and loving yourself will provide the strength to reject such tendencies.

Jesus Knew Whose He Was

Jesus also knew that he was the Son of God. Whether others believed it or not, it was a fact. He was secure in that relationship. That sense of security also enabled him to remain undaunted, despite the obstacles and challenges placed before him by those who failed to understand and believe. In his chapter in *The Gospel in Black & White* (1997), Deddo's exposition on the Trinity and racial reconciliation explores Christ's security. According to the author, our love for one another should parallel and emulate the love, mutuality and connectedness that exists between God, Jesus Christ and the Holy Spirit. Just as the Trinity represents an indelible relationship and cannot exist outside its tripartite structure, "humanity has its existence in and through personal relations" (1997, p. 59). Romans 8:14-15 confirms this relationship via our adoption into the heavenly family. We are also God's sons and daughters. We should have the same sense of security Christ had, even when we experience prejudices. Knowing that we are fearfully and wonderfully made (Ps 139:14) and created a little lower than the angels (Heb 2:7-8) substantiates our importance to God and our uniqueness—even in the face of those who would have us believe otherwise.

Jesus Knew His Purpose

Christ came to earth for a specific purpose: to enable humanity to be reconciled back to God. His mission was crucial to the fate of us all. As such, he remained focused. Recall his example of love, service, forgiveness and humility found in John 13. As Christ washed the disciples' feet, he was aware of his pending, agonizing death. He was also aware of the flawed nature of the men whose feet he washed. Peter would deny him, Judas would betray him, the rest would scatter in fear. Yet his purpose remained unchanged. The teaching/learning moment in John 13 meant that Christ would have to focus not on himself and his pending hardship but on illustrating servanthood to the disciples (Russell 2004). It didn't matter what others thought or said or how they behaved, as God's Son, he remained focused on his mission.

What is your purpose? Have you identified your spiritual gift(s) (1 Cor 12:28)? Is it teaching? Exhorting? Helps? Maybe you have been blessed with a discerning spirit? Do you use your gifts in ministry? What has God purposed for you to do with your life? Each of us has a spiritual gift. Some people have more than one. Determining your spiritual gift(s) may require in-depth self-examination, lots of prayer, fasting and meditation. Listening to the Holy Spirit will also be necessary. Some people realize their spiritual gift(s) at a young age (I knew I had the gift of teaching when I was about eight years old), and God reveals them to others later. Spiritual gifts become evident at different times for each individual, but knowing and using our gifts are central to our purpose in life. Having a sense of purpose also makes it easier to weather life's storms, no matter the source.

Jesus Knew the Source of Their Behavior

Christ was able to discern the hearts of those around him. He knew why the people thought, believed and acted as they did.[6] This knowledge enabled him to interact with them more effectively. Similarly, when we understand some of the reasons people may harbor prejudices (refer to chapter three), we are better able to address such situations with our peace intact. Some of you may be thinking, *Of course Jesus could rise above prejudices and find peace. He is God's Son. He's perfect, but I'm not!* Christ's temptation in the wilderness and his prayers on the Mount of Olives were two of the most challenging times in his life (Mt 4:1-11; Lk 22:39-46). But just as angels ministered to him during those trying life experiences, persons who face prejudices can look to God's Word for comfort. Scripture is full of examples of how Christ overcame obstacles and challenges for peace. Reading and meditating on such texts and putting them in action can help bring about similar results in our lives.

Jesus' unique ability to serve as the ideal biblical mentor rests in his exposure to the many everyday challenges we would face as people and

---

[6]The Gospels provide numerous examples of Jesus' ability to discern the hearts and minds of those around him. Refer to Mt 12:25-37; Mk 8:16-21; 9:10-14 and Lk 6:6-11 for a few examples.

as Christians. Relative to this book, his experiences provide an example of how God's power can be tapped to overcome a variety of negative circumstances, including prejudices and discrimination. Similarly, his experiences provide evidence that it is possible to lead a peaceful life, even in the midst of persons who misunderstand, mistrust and in some instances, hate us. Stassen and Gushee summarize it best: "Jesus fulfilled Isaiah's prophecy that peacemaking would be a key mark of the reign of God. Jesus taught, lived and died the way of peacemaking" (2003, p. 158). In addition, Jesus' sinless position on "both sides" of a potentially prejudicial encounter confirms that those who emulate his life and lifestyle can act as role models, in general, and when addressing prejudices, in particular.

READ ABOUT

- **How Christ Brings Peace:** John 14:27
- **Faith and Peace:** Luke 7:36-50; 8:41-48
- **God's Unbiased Nature:** Acts 10:34-38

5

Who Is Affected by Prejudices?

FOR POWER

Truly I tell you, just as you did it to one of the least of these who are members of my family, you did it to me.

MATTHEW 25:40

Do you remember the movie *It's a Wonderful Life?* In it the main character, George Bailey, was allowed to see what the world would be like had he not been born. After a series of shocking revelations, George realized that his life had directly and indirectly touched the lives of friends, family members, associates and even people he'd never met. Whether we realize or acknowledge it, our lives and our lifestyles, reflected in how we think, feel and act, also affect the lives of others. It might be difficult to realize the sheer magnitude of this truth—that each of us is able to affect the lives of others—positively or negatively.

Prejudices limit the God-given power of its bearers and can prevent recipients from having peace, but their effects are even more far-reaching. Who is affected by the bearers of prejudices? Who is negatively influenced by prejudices? Do prejudices only impact the people that harbor them or are others affected? Are the effects of prejudices always direct or can their effects be indirect? Do the responses of people who experience prejudices influence others? Although I have mentioned some persons and groups that are affected by prejudices in earlier chapters, it is important to clearly present those groups most influenced. This is the primary goal of this chapter. The reader will note that this chapter differs slightly from earlier chapters because the section "For Power" is substantially longer than the latter section, "For Peace." This is due to the nature of the chapter, which focuses on bearers of prejudices and the people they tend to harbor prejudices against. I also examine some of the persons that can be negatively influenced indirectly by prejudices. The final section considers how others are affected when they are exposed to the life testimony of recipients of prejudices (particularly Christians) who are unable to combat these negative encounters.

Groups Affected by Prejudices

Racial and ethnic groups. These groups probably come to mind most often as recipients of prejudices. According to 2002 census figures, about 13.4, 12.7 and 4.0 percent of the U.S. population is Hispanic, African American and Asian, respectively. Although over 70 percent of the United States is white, racial and ethnic minorities represent a substantial and growing segment of the population. Because most racial and ethnic minorities are visually distinguishable, they tend to stand out (for example, as the only African American in most of my graduate engineering classes, my presence and/or absence was always noticed). Given the number of books, articles, news reports and other materials on issues of race, ethnicity and reconciliation, it seems that we would have gotten this right by now. Some studies suggest that prejudice and discrimination based on race and ethnicity are on the decline; most disagree. Many scholars agree that this type of prejudice still exists, but has taken on new and different forms.[1] Some forms of prejudice against such groups are covert; other forms are institutionalized. (*Institutionalized discrimination occurs when organized, structured groups and processes result in unequal treatment and outcomes for certain groups. For example, if disparate educational systems exist in poor urban areas as compared to suburban areas such that children in the former areas receive a subpar education, institutionalized discrimination has occurred. Refer to research by Omi and Winant 1994; and Roediger 1991.) And these types of prejudices can have cumulative negative effects.

---

[1]A few studies on the subject are Geartner and Dovidio 1986; Gallagher 1999; and Kirschenman and Neckerman 1991.

Feagin, the noted scholar on racial and ethnic relations, makes the following observation concerning the African American experience that can be applied to other racial/ethnic groups:

> Particular instances of discrimination may seem minor to outside white observers when considered in isolation. But when blatant acts of avoidance, verbal harassment, and physical attack combine with subtle and covert slights, and these accumulate over months, years, and life times, the impact on a black person is far more than the sum of individual instances. . . . The micro-level events of public accommodations and public streets are not just rare and isolated encounters by individuals: they are recurring events reflecting an invasion of the microworld by the macroworld of historical racial subordination. (1991, pp. 114-15)

Christians are challenged to be watchful for blatant as well as more subtle forms of racial and ethnic prejudice. Here's an example.

After earning a graduate degree, my friend Karla began her search for employment. After a lengthy period and several positions "just to pay the bills," she found a position as an analyst in her field of study. Karla was so excited about finally being able to use her education and training in a meaningful way. The company was small and although she was one of only two African American employees, Karla felt comfortable in her new position. After working closely with her peers, Karla learned a startling truth. She was the only African American analyst—and the only analyst with a masters degree. Some of the white analysts did not have a college education at all. Yet they all held the same position and had the same salary; one white male even made more money! Was this just a coincidence or did the company have more stringent hiring standards for African Americans? Should she inquire and risk loosing her team-player image and possibly her job?

Let's look at another slightly different scenario. During a workshop on diversity I attended several years ago Peter spoke of the many stereotypes and prejudices associated with being of Asian decent. Everyone expects him to be a brain. In his college classes, he is expected to earn the highest grade on every paper, exam or quiz. If he doesn't (which is often), he can expect comments like, "I thought all you guys made straight A's." Peter is also expected to be reserved and quiet—a far cry from his talkative, outspoken nature. Many of his classmates treat him differently because he refuses to behave like *their* image of an Asian.

Studies show that Asians in the United States are often considered the model minority—more intelligent, more economically successful, less vocal and less threatening as compared to other minority groups. However, despite the achievements of large segments of the Chinese and Japanese populations, Asians are diverse and some experience poverty and discrimination (refer to work by Boswell 1986; Espiriti 1992; O'Hare, Frey and Fost 1994; Zhou 1992). Because of the image of the model minority, Peter must deal with preconceived notions about what it means to be Asian. He often feels that people don't really get to know him before deciding how he should act, feel and think. He considers himself an average student, more interested in sports than mathematics and science. But in school, he can't simply learn and have fun. Because he's trying to decide who *he* wants to be and become, Peter must often fight prejudices and stereotypes.

Although there are now laws in place against de jure forms of discrimination (for example, laws against segregation in schools and public places), it is harder to combat de facto discrimination (norms, "preferences," power relations and social customs that result in inequality). Throughout history, prejudice against various racial and ethnic groups has taken the form of assimilation, segregation and even genocide.

Karla and Peter's experiences reflect intergroup prejudice because they take place across different groups. Prejudice can also manifest *within* groups (referred to as intragroup prejudice) and among racial and ethnic groups in various ways. For example, intragroup prejudices can take the form of Cubans looking down on Puerto Ricans, lighter-skinned African Americans harboring prejudices against darker-skinned African Americans, whites from Germany discriminating against whites from Italy, and Japanese Americans devaluing Filipinos. In addition, as opposed to realizing their common problems, historically, oppressed groups have also harbored prejudices against each other. For example, Korean shop owners in urban areas have been known to exhibit prejudices against their African American customers (and vice versa) (Chen and Espiritu 1989; W. Wilson 1996). And the list can go on and on.

Males and females (sex/gender). Can women be ministers? Some male ministers say no. I once had a conversation with a pastor who supported this philosophy. This African American minister could accept women as exhorters, evangelists and Christian educators, but never as ministers. He quoted Scriptures to support his beliefs and commented that men should not be subject to women and that Christ never had a female disciple. In this instance, the minister was incorrectly applying 1 Corinthians 14:34-35 and 1 Timothy 2:11-12 to justify the exclusion of women from the clergy.[2] When I responded that Christ also never had an African American disciple, he only guffawed. No amount of discussion could change his mind. I found it difficult to understand how this same pastor could preach against racism while condoning sexism in his congregation. My interests in this topic spurred academic investigation that uncovered varied factors that result in the exclusion of female clergy—and support for such practices among Christian males as well as females. Factors other than sexism among males include theological beliefs that focus on the complementary nature of males and females based on certain prescribed gender roles, denominational beliefs, church tradition, hegemony among females, intragroup prejudices among females and gatekeeping among both males and females.[3]

Prejudice against women exists in other arenas as well. I have often been considered atypical because of my desire to pursue higher education. Even well-meaning relatives have their own ideas about what it means to be a woman. "Yes, get a good education Sandra, but not too much—most men don't like a really brainy woman." Or "You're just too independent. A man needs to feel like he's in control in a relationship." These types of comments reflect traditional gender roles. Generally speaking, gender roles are norms created in a given society about how people should think and act based on whether they are male or female.

---

[2]Several studies about women clergy include Chaves 1996, 1997; J. Grant 1989; Konieczny and Chaves 2000; Lincoln and Mamiya 1990; Townsend-Gilkes 2001; C. Tucker 1996; Wessinger 1996.

[3]S. Barnes (forthcoming), "Whosoever Will Let *Her* Come: Gender Inclusivity in the Black Church," *Journal for the Scientific Study of Religion*. This type of information and my seminary training and mentoring in a gender inclusive congregation has enabled me as an ordained minister to address situations when I am confronted by males (and females) who question the legitimacy of my calling. Persons who disagree with my stance as a minister are usually "politically correct" in their objections (quoting 1 Cor 14:34-35 and 1 Tim 2:11-12 or emphasizing the importance of male leadership). However, I have yet to experience a lull in requests for my ministerial assistance.

For example, "men" are often expected to be aggressive, hard, emotionless and intelligent. In contrast, as "women," females are often expected to be the opposite—submissive, soft, emotional and lacking intelligence. Although males and females are becoming more *androgynous (i.e., men who raise their children, women who work outside the home), traditional gender roles continue to be common in our society. Traditional gender roles suggest that women must accept certain roles in society or be socially penalized and also suggest that men are unable to relate to women who don't fit into a nice, simple box.

Readers are encouraged to reject such simplistic understandings about the rigidity of gender roles, either-or thinking and societal pressures to choose life paths based on the decisions and views of others. For example, during discussions in my sexuality and family courses, I encourage female students to pursue professional (careers) and personal goals (marriage) *if they so choose.* I also encourage male students to embrace more androgynous attitudes and behavior such that they can be receptive to females with nontraditional life views without feeling threatened. I encourage students to think "outside the box" and understand the possible benefits and drawbacks of more and less traditional gender roles, but to also realize that they have the ability to shape such decisions for themselves and work toward healthier relationships across sex/gender lines.[4]

Can prejudice also exist against men? For example, I've heard women complain that men don't show their emotions. These women wish their husbands and male friends would be more open—reveal their "inner selves"—even cry sometimes. But is this really what women want? Some of these same women will later complain about

---

[4]My suggestions do not reflect some naive belief in "superwomen" who can do it all, in females who must automatically choose between family and career, or in the existence of a barrage of males who will readily reject gender roles that studies show benefit them and their personal and professional pursuits. Nor does it ignore the reality that compromises must be made during various seasons in the lives of males and females. It is rather a challenge to make informed decisions rather than merely following societal dictates regarding gender roles; to avoid fears of reprisal if one rejects such roles and attempts to forge nontraditional ones; to acknowledge possible perks and/or penalties associated with the degree to which persons accept or reject such roles; and to realize that it is possible to be part of more gender-balanced relationships and interactions. And as Christians, because we know that God's power supercedes that in society, we are all the more compelled to think and behave in transformative ways.

"wimpy guys" who show *too much* emotion. I often think that it would be difficult to be a man and have to face some of society's definitions of masculinity. In "The Manhood Puzzle," David Wilmore (1995) agrees. According to Wilmore, men are expected to be protectors and providers. Society encourages them to think and behave in certain ways in order to prove that they are men. And even when the situation is dangerous or illogical (for example, fighting off a house intruder or protecting a woman's "honor"), men are expected to take the lead in ways that women are not. Wilmore also suggests that many men willingly take part in these situations. Is it acceptable for a man *not* to be the primary breadwinner in the family? What if a wife earns more money than her husband? What if a husband wishes to be the homemaker? How would you feel if your husband, father, son or male friend decided to quit his high-paying job to work on a worm farm in Kansas? Would you applaud his nontraditional zeal for life or suggest he seek counseling? Why should a man have to put himself in harms way as evidence that he's a man? We often are suspicious of or reject men who do not fit our stereotypical mold of manhood. This reflects a form of prejudice. We are actually saying, "Either you act like the rest of the men or you aren't acceptable." Other writers show that men and women are more likely to devalue their partners who do not meet an ideal model referred to as "Prince Charming" or "Cinderella" (Franklin and Pillow 1999). In these instances, preconceived expectations (usually unrealistic and biased) can result in devalued views about others and ill treatment of them.

The poor. "What do you want to be when you grow up?" If you asked a group of children this question, responses like teacher, doctor, lawyer, ballerina, pilot, cowboy, dentist or actor would be expected. I would wager that no child would say, "I want to be poor" or "I want to work two low-paying jobs and still be unable to pay my bills and take care of my family." And I suspect that none of the girls would say, "I want to be a welfare mother."

No one plans to be poor. However, the poor exist and their numbers are growing. Poverty takes place when persons lack acceptable amounts of money or material resources to meet their basic living needs. In the United States, poverty is determined based on the official poverty line developed in 1964 by the Social Security Administration.[5] The threshold is adjusted annually, but was about $19,484 for a family of four in 2004. In 2003, about 12.5 percent of the U.S. population lived in poverty. However, poverty affects groups differently. For example, poverty rates for African Americans and Hispanics were 22.4 and 22.5 percent in 2003, compared to 8.2 percent for whites and 11.8 percent for Asians and Pacific Islanders.[6] Poverty rates are highest for single-parent families. In 2003, only 5.4 percent of married-couple families and 13.5 percent of male-headed families lived in poverty. The rate was 28.0 percent for female-headed families. In 2003, about 19.8 percent of children under 6 were poor, but 52.9 percent of children younger than 6 who lived in female-headed families were impoverished. Research shows that minorities, women and children are most affected by poverty.[7]

Poverty is a result of many factors: social constraints, discrimination, lack of opportunity, poor decisions and limited training, to name a few. However, a common societal picture presents the poor as lazy, shiftless people who do not want to work but merely wish to be taken care of by the government. Contrary to this image, studies show that most poor people are employed (i.e., the *working poor), embrace mainstream attitudes and behavior regarding the importance of hard work and education, and strive to make a better life for themselves and their children.[8] In his groundbreaking article "Positive Functions of the Undeserving Poor" sociologist Herbert Gans (1994) argues that the poor play critical economic, social and cultural roles in society and that we as a nation are not seriously trying to end poverty. He argues that poor people meet various "functions" or objectives in society. For example, fewer social

---

[5]This threshold reflects a set of rock-bottom allowances based on estimated annual food expenditures. An individual is officially considered "poor" if his or her personal family income falls below this governmental standard. Factors such as deindustrialization, disparate marriage rates, residential discrimination and segregation, racism, unemployment and poor educational systems have contributed to continued poverty and racial differences in poverty rates.

[6]Although the poverty rate and number in poverty remained the same for African Americans between 2002 and 2003, the rate for Asians has increased from 10.1 percent in 2002. The actual poverty rate for Hispanics remained unchanged, but the *number* of poor Hispanics increased from 8.6 million in 2002 to 9.1 million 2003.

[7]The tendency for increased poverty among women and children are referred to as the feminization and juvenilization of poverty, respectively. Statistics from 2004 census data.

[8]There is a large body of literature on this subject. Refer to S. Barnes 2005; Jargowsky 1994; MacLeod 1995; Newman 1999; W. Wilson 1987, 1996.

workers and police officers would be needed if there were no poor people. In addition, the poor are needed to do the "dirty jobs" that the nonpoor don't want to do; they can be used as scapegoats for blame; and they provide a point of comparison for the nonpoor to gauge their "success." This means that in many instances, the existence of the poor helps the nonpoor feel better about themselves and lead more comfortable lives. Gans's list of functions of the poor suggests that the nonpoor, particularly those in power, are instrumental in maintaining poverty and could do more to address this social problem.

Why do some people harbor prejudices against the poor? When I was younger, as an unmarried engineer with no dependents, I used to get angry when I got my paycheck because 33 percent of my earnings went to taxes. And a percentage of taxes are used for government assistance. I thought, *A large portion of* my *hard earnings will go to people who don't even work! Get a job,* I thought. I was quickly convicted by the Holy Spirit that my well-paying job and the education and training needed to get such a job were gifts from God. I was blessed. I was also harboring prejudices against the poor based on a lack of information at that time.

Now I know that the reasons for and consequences of poverty are not simply explained or understood.[9] It's often easier to blame the poor than to work to understand their situations and render meaningful help. According to statistics, over 50 percent of all Americans are only two paychecks away from economic hardship. This means that for most of us if we become ill or hurt and are unable to work for one month, we could find ourselves in a financial bind. As it states in 1 Corinthians 15:10, "But by the grace of God I am what I am." Blaming persons in poverty is often easier than acknowledging our fears that many of us could easily be in their shoes.

Groups from different regions and locations. I have lived in a variety of places in the United States and also enjoy traveling to other countries. One of the challenges of traveling outside your comfort zone is to

---

[9]Refer to the structure vs. agency debate in sociology that suggests structural forces such as globalization, deindustrialization, historic and current discrimination, and segregation are the primary factors behind much of the poverty in the United States. The premise does not discount poor choices on the part of some economically disadvantaged, but tends to emphasize macrolevel factors more than individual choices to explain poverty (S. Barnes 2005; Jargowsky 1994, 1996; Massey and Denton 1993; W. Wilson 1987).

be open to new experiences and cultures—including different languages, foods and clothing—in new places. I referred to the term "cultural relativity" earlier in this book. When interacting with people from other areas, it is sometimes easy to view them ethnocentrically (based on our own cultural standards) as opposed to acknowledging diversity (based on cultural relativity) and appreciating differences that do not violate Christian dictates. Furthermore, it sometimes seems easier to do this when we are abroad rather than when we are in our own backyards. Prejudices against persons from different regions and locations can take many forms. This form of prejudice is often intermixed with other forms. For example, groups from other regions may be racial and ethnic minorities or they may be from a different socioeconomic position. Here are a few common examples.

Whites who live in rural areas (who are often poor or working class) are regularly the butt of comedic jokes on television. Although some comedians shy away from making jokes about racial and ethnic minorities, making fun of the experiences of "country hicks," "rednecks" and people who live in trailer parks are all too common, especially on late-night television. Although these jokes may seem harmless, this type of mentality can manifest in subtle prejudices. Furthermore, the term "ghetto-fabulous" has become popular lately to disparagingly describe the clothing, language, hairstyles and lifestyles of segments of urban (usually poor and working class) African America. Areas such as ghettos, barrios and slums[10] are often considered devalued and dangerous places, and such negative sentiment can easily become associated with the people who live there.

Mr. & Ms. Average Appearance. What does it mean to be physically attractive? Who determines the standard? Do Christians embrace the world's beauty yardstick? Many times, the answer is a resounding *yes*. A male associate once commented on his desire to find a mate. As a Christian, he wanted a Christian wife. She would also have to be pretty, intelligent, funny, family-oriented and down-to-earth. Only one thing turned

[10]Although *ghettos, barrios* and *slums* are separate terms used by Jargowsky (1994, 1996) and others to describe poor urban areas where large percentages of African American, Hispanic and whites live, respectively, mainstream society appears to associate urban poverty with the term *ghetto*.

him off: he would not date or marry an overweight woman. I found this quite interesting since he (judging by his size and girth) had to weigh almost 300 pounds. Studies show that people who meet society's traditional notions of attractiveness are assumed to have more desirable personalities, be more successful and be happier. (I use the term *traditional* to acknowledge that beauty is in the eye of the beholder and to remind readers that definitions of beauty vary across societies, cultures and time. Thus what is often considered beautiful in society is constantly changing, yet certain profiles are generally considered more beautiful than others.) Media representations place such high value on physical appearance that men often consider it the most important factor in potential mates (Buss 1989), and women are often preoccupied with their outward appearance at the expense of internal characteristics such as spirituality, intelligence and personality.[11] Remember the cartoons featuring the skinny guy on the beach? The muscular, burly guy constantly ridicules him. The thin guy does not defeat the muscular guy or get the girl (i.e., achieve success) until he "buffs up" and changes his physical appearance.

The media focus on the outward appearance can be emotionally, psychologically, spiritually *and* economically draining. According to information provided by the National Women's Health Information Centers (NWHIC), about 56 percent of women and 43 percent of men do not like their overall appearance.[12] According to the National Eating Disorders Association, 80 percent of women are dissatisfied with their appearance. Think about it: the average American woman is about 5' 4" tall and weighs 140 pounds; the average American model is about 5' 11" tall and weighs 117 pounds. This means that most fashion models are thinner than 98 percent of American women. And although fashion models weigh substantially less than the typical woman, they are often the standard by which many women evaluate their appearance. As a result, the diet industry is reported to be a $40 billion industry annually, and 25 percent of men and 45 percent of women are on a diet on any given day. Yet about 95 percent of all dieters regain the lost weight within one to five years (Crowther et al 1992; Fairburn et al 1993).

---

[11]Refer to Wolf's (1991) research on "beauty-minded" women.
[12]Taken from a 1996 survey.

The quest for the "perfect" appearance is taking its toll on children as well. Studies show that over 40 percent of elementary school children between first and third grade wish they were thinner (Collins 1991), and 80 percent of ten-year-olds are afraid of being fat.[13] Statistics also show that the cases of eating disorders among men and women are on the increase. Conservative U.S. estimates suggest that 5 to 10 million girls and women and 1 million boys and men have an eating disorder such as anorexia, bulimia, binge eating disorder or borderline conditions (Crowther et al 1992; Fairburn et al 1993). However, body size is just one component of the beauty-minded equation. The cosmetic industry is also a multibillion-dollar industry; we are bombarded with media ads for acne medicines, teeth whitening kits, thigh and buttocks lifters, slimmers and shapers, and fashions to make us appear youthful, sexy, successful and *happy*.

Persons who focus their attention on reaching society's ever-changing beauty standard are likely to be constantly displeased with themselves. They are also more likely to transfer similar sentiments to those around them who also deviate from the idealized standards. As a result, persons who weigh more, look different, dress differently, don't have "perfect" skin or seem to always have "bad hair days" may be devalued or treated unfairly (remember the court case when the airline carrier wanted to fire a competent flight attendant because they believed she was too large).

In addition, persons who do not meet society's standard of beauty may feel inferior. These feelings may affect their sense of self-worth, their outlook on life and how they relate to others. Instead of accepting themselves as God's creations, many opt to try to change their appearance—reality shows such as *Extreme Makeover* and *The Swan* illustrate this trend. Some women believe that makeup will do the trick. Some men wonder, *Maybe a toupee will help*. Given all these mixed messages, it becomes difficult for many to distinguish between proper eating habits, the need for exercise, an appropriate hygiene regimen and the importance of improving spiritually, intellectually and socially (i.e., things on the inside)—and an unhealthy focus on the outer appearance. Thus,

---

[13]Mellin et al. 1991. For a slightly different examination of the subject, refer to Thompson's (2002), "Eating Problems Among African American, Latina, and White Women."

having a healthy lifestyle gets lost in a never ending battle to avoid becoming a member of those groups that are directly or indirectly disparaged because of their outer appearance.

It is often difficult to convince people (especially the young), that we can harbor prejudices against others (and ourselves) based on appearance. A Bible story often gets the point across. In 1 Samuel 16, the Lord wishes to appoint a new king of Israel. King Saul has been rejected for failing to follow God's prophetic commands; a new king is needed. God sends the prophet Samuel to Bethlehem, to the house of Jesse, to anoint a new king. Initially, Samuel assumes the oldest son, Eliab, is the chosen one. However, God informs the prophet, "Do not look on his appearance or on the height of his stature, because I have rejected him; for the LORD does not see as mortals see; they look on the outward appearance, but the LORD looks on the heart" (1 Sam 16:7). The Lord did not select any of Jesse's first seven sons. It was the youngest, David, whom God had chosen to be the next king of Israel. Interestingly, the passage notes that David was "ruddy, and had beautiful eyes, and was handsome" (1 Sam 16:12). However, this was not God's criteria for selecting him. God knew David's heart—God knew that David would be a great king. Samuel anointed the young sheepherder as God commanded, and "the spirit of the LORD came mightily upon David from that day forward" (1 Sam 16:13). Just as God evaluates us based on our hearts, differences in the outer appearance become inconsequential when we do the same.

The elderly. You might think that charges of racial and ethnic discrimination are the most common cases filed at the Equal Employment Opportunity Commission (EEOC); you would be incorrect. Charges of ageism (discrimination based on age) are the most common cases. We live in a youth-oriented society. In many other cultures, the elderly are revered, respected and honored. Sadly, in the United States, the elderly are too often looked upon not as wise, experienced sages, but as burdens. For example, research by Butler (1975) shows that society often stereotypes the elderly as confused, helpless, unhappy and cantankerous. Society often associates youth with attractiveness, vitality, importance and *life*—so much so that many fear aging. For example, plastic surgeons have lucrative businesses; some people fear loosing their jobs as they age; and some women fear loosing their spouses to younger women.

Historically, the elderly in the United States were the most likely group to experience poverty, abandonment and crime—so much so that a group of them organized to promote unity among the elderly and to lobby for better treatment and improved living conditions. The Gray Panthers, as they were called, were instrumental in championing civil rights for the elderly and informing the larger society about an important segment of the community that had been devalued and ignored.[14] Today, efforts continue through organizations such as AARP to insure fair treatment of the elderly, and some media representations present the elderly in a more positive light.[15] Scripture tells us that Methuselah lived to be 969 years old (Gen 5:27). We don't know much about this biblical character, except that he lived a long life. However, I suspect that he had to be someone of importance for the writer to include a note about him in the text. I believe that Methuselah provides an example of the longevity of life in ancient biblical times and serves as a reminder of the importance of the elderly. To be honest, no matter who we are, time will eventually affect us all. If we appreciate the elderly, the time and wisdom and knowledge that can come as we age will be a welcomed guest and not a feared specter to evade.

Single people. Everything is better in twos! Going to the movies or a museum or out dancing seems more fun when done with a partner. Ever dine out and ask for a table for *one?* Vacations are even cheaper when purchased for two. For some people, being complete—being *whole*—means being two. This is often society's message to the single person, even though according to 2002 census figures, over 45 percent of U.S. adults are unmarried. The media is full of advertisements featuring happy couples doing happy-couple things. But some singles may be upset not because they are single but because others refuse to acknowledge singleness as an acceptable lifestyle. "All single women are looking for husbands." "Single men are looking for *all* women." "Singles are lonely." "Single people love to party." "Singles are irresponsible." I'm

---

[14]Refer to Sylvia Hewlett (1994) "Public Choices: Shortchanging the Future"; and Bengston, Marti and Roberts (1991) "Age-group Relationships: Generational Equity and Inequity" for research on the challenges faced by the elderly. For a contrasting perspective, refer to Samuelson (1988) "The Elderly Aren't Needy."

[15]The television show *The Golden Girls* was instrumental in showing the diverse experiences of older men and women and that the elderly can lead active, vital lives.

sure single readers have heard these and other similar comments. Such comments can be hurtful, but prejudices are all the more hurtful when they occur at the hands of other Christians.

I used to be a member of a very traditional, couples-oriented church. I enjoyed the Sunday church service and Bible studies and had many friends there. During conversations with some of the female single members, some noted the friendliness of many of the married males and the aloofness of their wives. After thinking about it, I had to agree. Some of the wives negatively confronted several single women who they felt were too friendly toward their husbands. Although the pastor attempted to address the issue, some contention still existed between certain wives and single women of the church. One recently married friend commented that although he had never been invited to dinner before, once married, he and his wife immediately became members of the "couples dinner circuit." Go figure.

Prejudices against unmarried persons can take the form of negative comments, stereotypes and suspicious attitudes. Some married persons may avoid single people. Married women may consider single women to be temptations to their husbands. Some consider single men to be less stable than married men. Others may look on single people with pity: obviously something must be wrong with them—they don't have a mate. I even know unmarried persons who avoid other singles for fear of being negatively labeled. It may seem overly critical, but I question the unequal benefits provided married couples and "twosomes" that are not afforded single persons, such as tax breaks and discounts on travel packages. Sometimes single people even buy into this same mentality. I recall being invited to a Christmas party hosted by a singles ministry at a local church. The entrance fee was $7.00 for singles and $10.00 for couples. I noted this unequal treatment (i.e., couples were given a $3.00 discount) to the ministry president and they agreed to change the fee—but initially they didn't realize that they were discriminating against the very group the activity was organized to support. Such inequities can make it difficult for those who are unmarried to joyfully embrace their lives as positive, purposeful and pleasing to God. Remember that Jesus Christ was single too.

Gays and lesbians. Are people born gay? Or do people choose to be gay? This has been an unending debate in academic as well as religious circles.[16] Persons who believe people choose to be gay are often less sympathetic toward the gay and lesbian community than those who support a genetic link to sexual orientation. Given the passion surrounding the topic, some Christians often steer clear of the topic for fear of being associated with a certain group, or when asked about the topic, they quote a few Scriptures (1 Cor 6:9 and the destruction of Sodom and Gomorrah in Gen 19), pray no one asks any other questions and quickly move to another subject. While research is inconclusive about the how and why surrounding diversity of sexual orientation, it is clear that homophobia and hate crimes inflicted on gays and lesbians are becoming more common. For example, research suggests that hate crimes based on sexual orientation are becoming more common in public places. Victims are often reluctant to report such experiences for fear of police bias or public disclosure of their sexual orientation or out of disbelief that the perpetrators will be punished.[17]

Gays and lesbians are often ostracized by family members and friends or may lose their jobs. Others have lost their lives. One news report suggested that 20-30 percent of teens who attempt suicide do so because they believe themselves to be gay or lesbian and have no one to whom they can turn. In some instances, Scripture is used to indirectly support the rejection of gays and lesbians who seek Christ and wish to be involved in a Christian community. Thus, although the church should be a safe haven or place of refuge, it is not available for all of God's creation. Christ came for us all. And he died for us all. We are challenged to see others as God sees us: as valuable and redeemable through the blood of Christ.

Other denominations and churches. Prejudice related to religion and church culture can be very subtle. It can take the form of inaccurate, often negative, beliefs and attitudes that discourage fellowship outside of

---

[16]A few seminal works in the Christian market include Comiskey (2003) *Strength in Weakness;* Davies and Gilbert (2001) *Portrait of Freedom;* and Jones and Yarhouse (2000) *Homosexuality: The Use of Scientific Research in the Church's Moral Debate.* Articles include Leland and Miller (1998) "Can Gays Convert?" and Wachs and Dworkin (1997) "There's No Such Thing as a Gay Hero." More recent academic work on African American gay and lesbian experiences can be found in Mays and Cochran (1999) and Cochran and Mays (1999).

[17]Green, Strolovitch, Wong and Bailey 2001; and Herek, Cogan and Gillis 2002.

one's denomination or religious affiliation. This type of prejudice prevents Christians from understanding and appreciating how others worship God and fellowship. "Those Baptists make too much noise during worship service." "I fell asleep during that Methodist service; talk about dull." "Unlike the so-and-so's, *our* church believes in education and community outreach." Some churches and denominations spend more time critiquing and judging each other than doing the work of the church.

In his book *What Makes You So Strong?* Rev. Dr. Jeremiah Wright (1993) identified two major church categories. He labeled them "mass churches" and "class churches." Mass churches consist mainly of working class people—postal workers, domestics, repairpersons, secretaries and custodians—the average "Joe and Josephine" off the street. Their church services tend to be emotional and lengthy. In contrast, class church members are primarily more formally educated—teachers, doctors, lawyers, nurses and engineers. Their church services are typically shorter in length and more formal. Dr. Wright suggests that mass members believe they worship God more freely and genuinely. They often consider class churches to be uppity. On the other hand, class church members feel that they worship God in a more humble, reverent manner. Some consider the mass churches too worldly and noisy (notice any subtle prejudices). He concludes that ideally churches should consist of mass as well as class—many types of people: the educated and the uneducated, those with *old* money, *new* money and *no* money, varying races and ethnic groups and backgrounds, all bound together in unity. All Christian denominations and churches have the same fundamental purpose: to praise and worship God, show love to others and reach the unsaved. Methods, creeds, doctrines and styles may differ, but there is still "One Lord, one faith, one baptism" (Eph 4:5).

Interracial/multiracial persons (interethnic/multiethnic persons). Although I've presented information about racial and ethnic minorities earlier in this chapter, I think it is important to recognize the unique challenges *interracial, *multiracial, *interethnic and *multiethnic persons may face. Because our society is becoming more racially and ethnically diverse, people now interact with others outside their specific racial and ethnic group more frequently. As such, the rates of dating and marriage across racial and ethnic lines are on the increase. Studies suggest that between 1 percent and 3 percent of couples today are interracial.[18] The increase in racial and ethnic diversity in the United States even prompted census officials to include special categories on the recent census surveys to capture these new forms of diversity. However, persons from mixed unions often find it difficult to fit in with a society that encourages dichotomies (i.e., black *or* white, Asian *or* Hispanic, African American *or* German American). People who are somehow considered "in between" may find themselves being asked to choose between their varied racial and ethnic heritages and later considered suspect for the choices they make.

In her book *Check All That Apply: Finding Wholeness as a Multiracial Person,* Sundee Frazier (2001) recounts these types of challenges: isolation from both African American and white society, being embraced by some whites but knowing they did not feel as accepting of other African Americans, coming to understand God's plan for her life—and how her journey toward forging a multiracial identity has provided unique insights into appreciating diversity in herself and others. Similarly, the book *Black, White, Other* by Lise Funderburg (1994) vividly and candidly presents the many challenges and pains associated with living in society as a multiracial or multiethnic person. The ethnographic analysis profiles persons for whom being "different" has affected their formative years in school, where they live, personal and business relationships, views about politics and, ultimately, how they make sense of life. Most have had painful experiences at the hands of others who have difficulty accepting mixed-race or mixed-ethnicity persons or who directly or indirectly embrace antimiscegenation (rejection of race-mixing, especially between whites and blacks) (Funderburg 1994; Aldridge 1989; Crowder and Tolnay 2000; Tucker and Mitchell-Kernan 1990). Each person in Funderburg's book can be considered successful in his or her own right, but considers him or herself most successful because of the strides they have made in accepting and embracing their varied heritages. Although

[18]Billingsley (1992) suggests that diverse persons are more likely to meet at the workplace and form personal relationships there based on common goals, objectives and work interests. In addition, regional differences exist in interracial relationships; more interracial unions are found on the West Coast and fewer in the southern Bible belt. Lastly, the most common types of interracial unions are between African American males and white females and white males and Asian females.

the last bans on interracial marriage were outlawed in June of 1967, social mores still make it difficult for many racially and ethnically mixed persons to be readily accepted.

"The Other." Although I've presented those groups I believe most commonly experience prejudice, the list should, in no way, be considered exhaustive. As such, this subsection includes the broad category of persons and groups often considered undesirable and who may directly or indirectly experience prejudice or be disparaged in society. I refer to the group as "the Other" because I contend that they represent persons who are, in some way, different or perceived to be different from members of the larger society and differ from the previously presented groups. "The Other" includes persons such as the drug-addicted, mentally ill, the incarcerated or previously incarcerated, the underclass, the homeless and prostitutes. It should be noted that persons from earlier mentioned groups may also be included in this category. For example, studies show that a disproportionate percentage of young male African Americans are incarcerated or that, by and large, most prostitutes are not "bad" women, but rather poor women. "The Other" generally includes persons who are on the fringes of society, are severely socially and/or economically isolated from the larger society or are considered dangerous. Many are persons for whom continued traditional interventions (for example, via social workers, community organizations, churches) have been unsuccessful. I know from personal experience.

Several years ago, during my stint as the secretary at a Baptist church in Atlanta, I was interrupted from my usual mundane Friday work by a church childcare worker. A woman had come in for assistance. The pastor had not yet arrived and, as a minister, I was the next logical person sought out. When I met the young lady, I could not believe my eyes. Deena's frail, emaciated frame barely seemed to sustain her, her eyes were sunken in and her skin sallow. She was disheveled, crying and begging for assistance. As I and another female minister sat with her, she mentioned that she was hungry. As she hurriedly ate some of the extra snacks from the daycare center, I noticed her persistent scratching, her glassy eyes and slurred speech. Although I am not specifically trained in this area, it was clear to me that Deena was drug addicted and suffering from withdrawal symptoms. She had come to the church for assistance to get away from her boyfriend (who was also her pimp) and to get into a drug treatment program. Such cases were usually referred to a special church ministry or to the pastor. However, the pastor had not arrived and a ministry representative could not be located; I and the other minister decided to intervene.

After calling what seemed like dozens of drug-rehabilitation programs, we finally found one that agreed to take Deena free for a thirty-day period based on the church's recommendation. Next, she needed to get some clothes; so the three of us traveled to her apartment. In retrospect, this was probably not a great idea because her boyfriend/pimp had threatened to kill Deena if she attempted to leave him. However, we had to get her to the facility by the end of the day or she would have to wait several weeks to enter. So we snuck into the apartment and hurriedly grabbed as many clothes as we could. All the while, I was praying that her boyfriend/pimp would not show up. We finally got Deena checked into the drug rehabilitation facility. I was relieved. I also felt a great deal of accomplishment: this was *real* ministry. Although I had not been able to do any of my typical church secretarial work, I felt good for doing the work of the church. But my sense of accomplishment was short-lived.

The following Monday, I was called into the pastor's office. He had received several telephone calls from Deena. She had left the drug-rehabilitation facility and was now back with her boyfriend/pimp. She was also livid. She accused me and the other minister of going into her apartment and stealing her clothes. She wanted the church to reimburse her for "the robbery" and us to be sanctioned. *This is the gratitude I get,* I thought. Although the pastor did not believe Deena's story and commended my motives, he did strongly dissuade my taking part in such activities in the future. Other Christians that I told about the situation were not as objective: "You should know not to mess with those crack-heads." "Did you think she was actually going to stay in rehab? She was just trying to scam the church for money to buy more drugs." "You should just leave *those people* alone." I don't know what ultimately happened to Deena. She disappeared as quickly as she had appeared. The experience made some members of the church hesitant to extend assistance to the chemically dependent. For others, it confirmed the futility of interventions for *those people*. And it became clear to me how easy it can be to write off such persons from society.

The unsaved. When we accepted Christ, our lives changed for the better. Looking back, we can't imagine how or why we lived without him in our lives. No matter what we experience, we have the assurance that God will take care of us. This often makes it difficult to understand why the unsaved refuse to accept Christ. We wonder, *Don't they understand who he is? Don't they realize how he can transform their lives? Why do they choose to remain in sin?* Some Christians may view the unsaved as heathens without morals and values, wallowing in sin—and liking it.

While dressing at a gym, I overheard a conversation between two women, one Christian, the other non-Christian. The former began to fervently witness to the latter, who seemed uninterested. After listening, the non-Christian woman calmly and quietly stated that she was leery of Christianity because she felt it was used to oppress women. She further noted her suspicions about male-dominated churches. I sat quietly, looking forward to hearing how the Christian would address the issues of this skeptical unbeliever (maybe I would learn some witnessing tips, I thought). Neither of us was prepared for the Christian woman's response. She began a tirade about feminism and the evils of "women of the 90s." Her voice escalated as she quoted Scriptures mingled with curses and made accusations about the possible sexual orientation of the non-Christian woman. In response, the non-Christian woman merely stared at her and hurried out of the dressing room. I was stunned. The Christian woman's comments revealed hidden prejudices masked by so-called spiritual fervor. She looked to me for validation; I did not comply.

Effectively witnessing to the unsaved means withholding accusations and personal judgments. It means refraining from considering ourselves spiritually superior. Nor should the unsaved be avoided or rejected for refusing to accept our beliefs. Sometimes we may indirectly scorn the unsaved and become impatient with them because they do not readily respond to our evangelical efforts. Our challenge is to continue to show love and respond to their needs as we are lead by the Holy Spirit. Most Christians possess great zeal when attending church: we love to sing, pray and fellowship—with each other. It is easy to minister to one another. However, we may fall short in our attempts to reach the unsaved.

Prejudices against the unsaved may manifest in subtle contempt for them or beliefs that they are somehow "the Other." Scripture challenges us to hate sin but love the sinner, but prejudice can result in hate for the former *and* the latter.

Others Negatively Influenced by Prejudices

In this section I focus on groups and persons who may not experience prejudice but who can be negatively affected by exposure to prejudicial comments and acts. For such persons—children, families, the unsaved and the larger society—prejudice can act as stumbling blocks to their growth as citizens and as Christians.

The children and family. I used to be the director and pianist of the Sunbeam Choir of children ages one to seven years old. My many hats of responsibility included director, accompanist, nose wiper, bathroom monitor, referee, offering distributor, arm and headrest, and disciplinarian. This last hat required me to watch the children constantly. I didn't know it, but they were also watching me. Each Sunday, church service ended as the congregation, with eyes closed, recited a benedictory statement. As we spoke in unison, we would raise our right hands. Instead of simply raising my right hand, I always made a peace sign (two fingers raised). One Sunday after benediction, I opened my eyes to find an entire row of Sunbeams holding up peace signs. Although it was amusing, it also showed me that even the smallest action can affect the thoughts, beliefs and actions of children.

Prejudicial words, comments and actions can slip out when we're around our children and other family members, or they may be exposed to prejudices through our friends and family. Can't you hear children saying, "If Daddy says it, it must be okay." "If Mommy does it, so can I." Many people say that I look just like my mother. I do resemble her, but my older sister seems like her carbon copy. Just as parents can pass on physical features and medical conditions to their children, they can also pass on prejudices. We are not born with prejudices. They are learned. Just as children emulate mannerisms and styles, they can pick up our feelings, attitudes and beliefs about others. For example, seminal work by George Herbert Mead (1962) illustrates how people develop the "self" through the process of imitation, play, games and taking on the "generalized other." Mead found that during their formative years children imitate or take on the roles of others around them.

Children often witness our actions firsthand. When little Jack's dad comments that "real men don't cry," what message does this send to Jack when life's challenges make him cry? Little Jan loves her new neighbors; she's waited so long to have kids her age to play with. She also likes the fact that they are all so different: Rena is Hispanic, Amber is African American, and Martin is from Pakistan. But Jan overhears her parents discussing the "changing neighborhood." They later tell her of their plans to move. "No," Jan shouts, "I've finally made friends!" What message are Jan's parents sending to her?[19] Prejudices are learned; it is often easier to learn positive beliefs, attitudes and behavior than it is to *unlearn* bad ones.

There are so many stresses on today's families—finding time to spend together, bills, jobs, college funds, braces, to name a few. Some tension is expected as the family attempts to stay together in the midst of societal and personal challenges (Newman 1988, 1993). Exposure to prejudices or failure to have candid conversations on the subject can result in added family tension. Sociologist Andrew Billingsley (1992) encourages African American parents who wish to rear emotionally and psychologically healthy children to practice "racial socialization." This process involves explaining the child's "double consciousness"—the fact that he or she is both of African and American descent—and the potentially negative and positive effects of these dual roles. I believe Billingsley's assessments apply to other groups as well and can be used to initiate conversations with children and family members about diversity in general. Without such conversations, family members are likely to learn whatever they "know" about diverse groups from the media, peer groups and sources that may or may not be accurate or objective.

Let's consider an example. If Dan doesn't care for *those people,* then Dan's wife Julie will have difficulty meeting and making friends with *those people*. Dan's son Greg would probably never date or marry one of *those people* even if he wanted to. Dan's daughter Christy will tend to

[19]Studies suggest the tendency toward "white flight" when an increasing number of racial and ethnic minorities, especially African Americans, enter predominately white neighborhoods (Anderson 1997; Drake and Cayton [1945] 1962; Roediger 1991).

shy away from *those people* when she meets them at school or play: "maybe Dad is right about *those people*." But what if Julie does not hold Dan's beliefs? How can she teach her children differently? Is it worth bringing another stress into the family? In this example, the beliefs and actions of an entire family have been affected by the prejudice of one member.

The unsaved. What if my Christian associate who was only attracted to "thin women" had made that comment in front of non-Christians? What would they have thought? Do our prejudices hinder God's message from reaching the unsaved? Remember my gymroom experience with the Christian and non-Christian. The Christian woman was quite rude and abrasive to a woman who only wanted answers to some very valid questions. When the unsaved woman left the gym, how do you think she felt about Christians? Did she see us as loving, kind persons interested in answering her questions and addressing her concerns? Or did she consider us to be dogmatic and downright mean? Hopefully, she saw her experience as an isolated case and didn't believe all Christians behaved that way.

Why would she base her opinions about all Christians on one experience? you may be asking. That's not fair. *She shouldn't let one bad experience prejudice her against all Christians.* But this how many prejudices develop. Whether the unsaved choose to accept Christ or not, many are watching us. Some watch us in hopes of catching us in sin that can be used against our ministry. Others are skeptical and watch us for evidence that we live the life we speak about. Some are at the brink of accepting Christ and watch us for an opportunity to ask, "tell me about the God you serve." Christians have a great responsibility. We are challenged to represent Christ wherever we go; God's message often depends on it.

I have attempted to present groups most often affected by prejudicial attitudes and behavior. I have also noted

READ ABOUT

- **Accountability to God:** Matthew 25:31-46; Hebrews 10:19-39
- **A Challenge to Love:** Hebrews 13:1-3; Ephesians 4:31—5:2
- **A Challenge for Holiness:** Ephesians 4:17-24; Hebrews 12:14

groups that can be indirectly influenced by prejudice. What other groups can you think of that are affected by prejudices? I'm sure you'll agree that few escape its effects. Some people are affected daily, others less frequently, but everyone is affected.

FOR PEACE

Let us then pursue what makes for peace and for mutual upbuilding. . . . It is good not to eat meat or drink wine or to anything that makes your brother or sister stumble.

ROMANS 14:19, 21

If you are a member of one of the groups presented in the first section of this chapter, your peace has probably been undermined as a result of prejudices. Prejudice means that differences are accentuated for negative reasons. And being a member of more than one of any of these groups—women who are members of a minority racial group, poor white women, "overweight" single people, unsaved gays and lesbians—can result in potentially compounded negative effects. But you decide to handle prejudices yourself, your way. You become indifferent. Or angry. Or fearful. You allow your life to be negatively altered by the attitudes, beliefs and behavior of others. Your quality of life, personal testimony and potential relationships are diminished. You are unable to find *real* peace. God wants to give you more power, but you aren't ready. You've faced prejudices and they've taken their toll.

Others Negatively Influenced by Unsuccessful Dealing with Prejudices

But recipients of prejudices aren't the only persons affected. Yes, prejudices can rob them of peace, but others can be affected as well. What other lives are directly or indirectly touched when recipients grapple with prejudice unsuccessfully? The reader will note that this section differs from earlier parallel chapters. My goal is not to ignore the very real reality of the negative results of prejudice on recipients' lives (additional information and interventions are provided in chapters six and seven). The goal here is to slightly shift the frame of reference toward persons and groups *associated* with persons who experience prejudices. In doing so, I hope to illustrate the transformative influence that recipients of prejudices can have not only in their own lives as recipients but also in the lives of others.

New Christians. Scripture informs us that new Christians are fed spiritual milk (1 Cor 3:2). As babes in Christ, they must grow and develop before they can digest spiritual meat. A young man once testified that since he had given his life to Christ trouble seemed to follow him wherever he went. His friends left him; bad things began to happen to him. He felt like a "trouble magnet." He just seemed to have bad luck. A seasoned Christian explained to the young man that when he was unsaved, Satan didn't need to bother him—he already had him. But now that he was a Christian, Satan would be after him, trying to get him to turn from his newly confessed life.

New Christians need much support, encouragement and guidance. They need to be helped to understand what it means to follow Christ. More importantly, they need to *witness* God's transforming power in our lives. By looking at us, new converts should see God in action. But when *seasoned* Christians live downtrodden, negative lives, how are new Christians affected? Probably negatively. When new converts fail to see God working through us, Christ in us and the Holy Spirit guiding us, it may become difficult for them to believe that the Trinity can transform them and their lives.

The unsaved. "Why should I join church? Christians act worse than sinners." How often have we heard this critique from the unsaved. Sadly, sometimes it's true. They may choose to reject Christ, but the unsaved are looking at us. Most of us can admit that when we were without Christ, we were drawn to him by the life testimony of a Christian. That's how witnessing generally works. Our personal testimonies are crucial. Have you ever talked to a bitter, angry Christian? Every comment was full of resentment and sadness. Some are ambivalent. Some constantly complain about the treatment of others. Rarely do they end the conversation with a testimony about how God delivered them. Or how the Holy Spirit comforted them or how Scripture gave them strength and peace. Or how they actually took action to address a problem based on the guidance of the Holy Spirit. Some can readily quote Scripture, but don't appear to apply it in their everyday lives. You wonder, *is this what it means to be a Christian?* The unsaved may wonder too. When the unsaved see us and we are dejected, depressed and downtrodden because of prejudices, it affects our testimony. Don't we say that God is able to do anything but fail? Can't God deliver us from adversity? Isn't God able to give us peace and strength to weather any storm? Isn't God able to transform situations and people so that believers are victorious? Isn't God able to give us the ability to confront such problems rather than complacently accept them? This is the type of testimony we are challenged to give.

I am not suggesting that persons who experience prejudice should "just deal with it" and cheerfully accept poor treatment. Such an attitude only serves to silently condone prejudicial attitudes and behavior. As we fight against prejudices, we should do so with a victorious spirit, strengthened in the knowledge that God is working through us and in us to end prejudices. A gospel song encourages Christians, "Don't wait till the battle is over, shout now. You know in the end, you're gonna win." This is the type of attitude that will help the unsaved understand the peace, joy, courage, strength and victory only possible through a relationship with Christ. Many non-Christians make excuses for refusing to surrender their lives to Christ. Some will never accept him. Some non-Christians may continue to reject Christ because of our behavior. But others are skeptical. They are unsure, but open to the possibilities. Our lives are often the only examples they will see to help them decide.

Children and the family. Children seem to see and hear everything. How often have you made a comment or gesture that you thought went unnoticed, but your child witnessed it? How often have you set a standard, fallen short and been reminded of it by little Johnny? "Do as I say and not as I do" seems somehow unacceptable in such instances. If we make comments or behave negatively because of past prejudicial experiences, we risk exposing our children to these negative emotions. In the movie *Guess Who's Coming to Dinner,* a young interracial couple sought the blessing of both sets of their parents before getting married. Both mothers eventually became receptive, but the fathers were not. In the final conversation between the African American character and his father, the son acknowledges the pain his father experienced due to prejudice and racism. He also confirms and reaffirms his love for his father. But he refuses to allow his father's bitterness to prevent him from marrying the woman he loves. Although this is just a movie, its implications are telling in terms how entire families can be affected by prejudices (and can affect others as well).

Let's use the example from earlier in this chapter in another way. Dan has experienced prejudices at the hands of *those people.* If Dan doesn't care for *those people,* then Dan's wife Julie will have difficulty meeting and making friends with *those people.* Dan's son Greg would probably never date or marry one of *those people* even if he wanted to. Dan's daughter Christy will tend to shy away from *those people* when she meets them at school or play: "Maybe Dad is right about *those people.*" But what if Julie does not hold Dan's beliefs. How can she teach her children differently? Is it worth bringing another stress into the family? In this example, the beliefs and actions of an entire family have been affected by those of one member.

Just as parents can pass on prejudices to their children, parents who have faced prejudices can pass on the negative effects. Earlier in this chapter, I noted Billingsley's (1992) assessment that many African American families *socialize their children to be cognizant of how being of African and American descent can influence their lives. He suggests that parents who fail to do so indirectly make it difficult for their children to live well-adjusted lives in a predominately white society. "Double consciousness" also means instilling in children a positive racial and ethnic identity and encouraging them to interact with many diverse groups and evaluate persons based on their character and not their color. Racial socialization also includes the sobering message to children that they may experience prejudices and discrimination because they are different. The author suggests that having such conversations within the safety of the home and with caregivers can make potentially sensitive topics less harrowing and better prepare children for the positive and negative experiences they may face.

I believe that Billingsley's findings can be applied to other groups that may experience prejudices such that, for example, poor and working class parents can explain class-based challenges their children may face, parents can discuss gender roles and ways to avoid gender-based prejudices, or parents can instill a sense of pride in their children, no matter their weight or size. We love our children and other family members and want to protect them. This means providing the nurturing and godly instruction needed to prepare them for the challenges they may face in life. This also includes helping them develop positive attitudes and behavior toward others.

People who look up to us. When I was about thirteen, I began teaching the nursery class in Sunday school. I was so proud. I memorized all the children's names, even though there were often twenty-five students, diligently prepared my lesson plans and never missed a session. One day, a church deacon commended me on my hard work. His daughter was one of my students. He commented that she was always mentioning something I'd said during class: "Miss Sandra said this . . . or Miss Sandra said that . . . Your instruction in Sunday school kept us both in line," he laughed. Just as students from my class looked up to me, others look up to us. Sometimes we are unaware that persons are emulating us. How we respond to prejudices can impact their choices if they ever face similar situations.

People who are prejudiced. My mother worked closely with a white coworker named Tim for almost twenty years. Their company had gone through many changes during that period—reorganizations, downsizings and management changes—but they always seemed to somehow come through with their jobs intact. Despite very different backgrounds and religious beliefs, they had become good friends. Tim was somewhat hot-tempered, and my mother was the still, calming voice that seemed to quiet the storm. One day Tim was in a nasty mood. Mom was the closest person in the line of fire, so he took his frustrations out on her. This included yelling and making a racial remark. When I heard about his remarks, I was furious. But my mother explained that although Tim had been wrong and she had initially been upset, she had forgiven him. She did not condone Tim's remarks nor did she let them go without stern comment. Mom had a long, hard talk with Tim, during which she told him how hurt she had been by his remarks and that if they were going to remain friends, he could *never* speak to her that way again. She did not downplay Tim's responsibility in the encounter nor exonerate his wrong comments and behavior. But she was able to handle the situation in a Christlike way. Though my mother and Tim no longer work together, they still remain friends.

How do you think Tim *expected* her to react? I bet he was surprised and shocked by her behavior. When Christians are faced with prejudices and we return tit for tat, we fail to represent Christ. We also provide persons who are prejudiced with additional ammunition for future encounters. Don't misunderstand me, I am not minimizing the role and choices played by prejudiced persons. Their actions and beliefs are wrong and they are responsible for them. But we can help the situation by refusing to be drawn into no-win encounters. Their prejudices limit them, but we don't have to let them limit us. It's just not worth it. Again, I am not suggesting that persons complacently accept poor treatment. Prejudices should be addressed—but in a godly manner. A godly response to prejudiced actions and comments may convict persons who harbor prejudices to change their ways. If not, we can still be content in the knowledge that we handled the situation in a godly way. We might not be aware of it, but the negative effects of prejudices can be devastating and far-reaching—if we allow them to be. If we allow prejudices to get the best of us, we begin to focus on self and away from our Christian purpose. We tend to lose control and forget that God is in control. Just as Christ's life can touch the lives of all of humanity, our lives touch and affect others. How will you impact the lives of others? Will you be plagued by prejudices or a victorious vessel for Christ? What will be your legacy?

READ ABOUT

- **Christian Challenges:** Luke 6:27-36; Romans 12:9-21; Hebrews 13:1-3

Confronting Prejudices

FOR POWER

For our struggle is not against enemies of blood and flesh, but against the rulers, against the authorities, against the cosmic powers of this present darkness, against the spiritual forces of evil in the heavenly places.

EPHESIANS 6:12

Have you ever watched a wrestling match? It can be a shock to the senses. Two great big burly guys with names like Killer Kelly or Dr. Destruction stalk each other in a ring. The wrestlers, usually dressed in wild costumes, hurl words of doom at each other, predict each other's painful demise and flex miles and miles of muscles. And all the while, a crowd of cheering, jeering, clapping and stomping fans egg them on. But these types of wrestling matches are a far cry from the spiritual wrestling that Christians may experience daily. Unlike professional wrestlers, our match doesn't end in a few hours after the final bell sounds. Ours is a continual one, between good and evil—and with much higher stakes. Similarly, prejudicial encounters represent a potential match between opposite forces. Refusing to give in to prejudices and their related ills reflects good; succumbing to them results in negative consequences.

In this chapter I specifically examine ways in which Satan, societal pressures and human nature are potentially involved in a prejudicial encounter, and I offer strategies to diffuse these situations. We can theologically debate the impetus of prejudices (i.e., some Christians would contend that Satan is the ultimate conspirator in such encounters and reduce explanatory factors solely to him). However, the Bible provides evidence that satanic influences as well as pressures from the world and the flesh (selfish motivations) are all possible sources of temptations to consider, understand and combat.

If we think or act based on prejudices, what's really happening? The bearer and the recipient appear to be the key players, but is this *really* the case? What other dynamics are influencing the situation? In order to appropriately handle the situation when facing prejudices, it is important to understand exactly what's occurring and the potential factors and forces involved. Earthly factors such as social pressures to conform to existing prejudices and "isms" in the world, indifference and complacency, as well as other factors presented in earlier chapters foster and perpetuate prejudices. These societal forces should not be underestimated or ignored. Research consistently illustrates the potential influence that macrolevel forces have on persons. In some cases, these influences are so pervasive we may not even be aware that (and how) they are shaping our attitudes and behavior (Billingsley 1992). For example, historically, because of prevailing societal dictates, it was acceptable to own slaves, to pay women employees less than men for doing the same job, and even to allow children to work long hours under horrible employment conditions. Societies change and these types of practices are unacceptable and against the law in most instances. Many of the factors outlined in chapter three that are correlated with prejudices are the result of societal forces. Sadly, similar dynamics still occur today.

Furthermore, our own sinful human nature, what Scripture refers to as the "flesh," can shape how we feel and think and what we do (or refrain from doing) in regard to prejudices. Even Christians can succumb to peer pressure or their own self-interests and downplay or ignore prejudice-based injustices that occur in society. It becomes easy to think, *Why should I get involved? How does it benefit me? I may experience backlash if I actively work to fight prejudices. What have* those people *done for me? My life is hectic enough, I'll just pray that God will intervene.* We've been told to look out for Number 1—and this mentality can engender self-centeredness. Even rugged individualism can foster a sense of self-interest that undermines connectedness and community if not monitored soberly. Whether and how we make decisions—the choices we make—are determined by human agency. However, it is important to recognize that spiritual factors are also the impetus behind some prejudices.

Both the victims of prejudices and those who harbor prejudices may also be confronting Satan's influence. This chapter addresses three primary factors—Satan, the world and the flesh—that can influence a prejudicial encounter between the two parties. People act on prejudices, but prejudices stem from attitudes and beliefs—things we can't touch. Ephesians 6:12 reminds us that Christians wrestle against that which we cannot see or touch. Christians are embattled with demonic forces wrought by Satan, and attitudes and beliefs that fuel prejudices can originate from satanic influence as well. A professional wrestler can see his foe—he's the 300-pound man charging him. Spiritual wrestling is not as simple. When unprepared to address prejudices, we risk falling prey to Satan, the world or our own self-interests and becoming involved, not as Christians representing God and that which is good, but as participants in attitudes and actions that displease God. We all make choices. Harboring and acting on prejudices can only occur if we *choose* to do so. But it's often more complicated than we might think. Even the best of us can become part of a game of "divide and conquer" that prejudices can engender.

My mother's experience with her white coworker Tim reminded me of this fact (see chapter five). This incident illustrates the subtle nature of some prejudices and the importance of self-reflection and constant self-control. Tim's yelling at my mother and his racial remark in a fit of temper illustrate how it is possible to interact positively with diverse groups in settings such as places of employment, but harbor prejudices that emerge during conflict or result when perceived group position is questioned (Blumer 1958). When my mother told me what had happened during Tim's outburst, I was outraged: *What a jerk!* I thought. *How dare he talk to* my mother *like that. The woman is a saint! She had been his confidant through his many personal problems and family crises. And this was the thanks she got!* I wanted to call and give Tim a piece of my mind—and I wouldn't be as nice as my mother had been. She did not appear unduly angry, but no need, because I was angry enough for the both of us!

My mother's explanation to me reflected the wisdom of spiritual maturity. Although Tim had been wrong and she had initially been upset, she had forgiven him. She realized that he hadn't really meant what he said *(sure he had,* I thought, *he said it!).* Tim had succumbed to temptation. My mother's conversation with Tim didn't excuse or overlook the hurtfulness of his remarks. Remember, she said that if they were going to remain friends, Tim could *never* speak to her that way again. She did not downplay his responsibility in the experience nor excuse his hurtful statements and actions. But because she realized the reality of temptation and its possible sources, my mother was able to handle the situation in a Christlike way and she and Tim could remain friends.

The unsaved may be unaware of the source of their prejudicial thoughts and feelings or what motivates them to act on them. Christians may be aware of the truth, but few want to admit the ability to be tempted. But in order to effectively address prejudices, they have to be placed in the proper spiritual context. Just as God convicts us to do good, so too Satan, society and self may attempt to sway us to do the opposite (for example, Satan's job is to "steal, kill and destroy" and he's good at it). We are not prepared for spiritual wrestling by ourselves. However, Scripture directs us to "put on the whole armor of God, so that you may be able to stand against the wiles of the devil" (Eph 6:11). Furthermore, because we are also in the world, but not of it, Christians are challenged to be aware of society's ability to influence us. It is also important to remember the myriad of biblical examples when men and women of God chose to follow their own dictates concerning a matter—even when God had instructed them otherwise (remember Jonah?). Confronting prejudices is usually easier to discuss than to do, especially when we seem to be bombarded by them. But in order to fight prejudices spiritually, our primary weapons for battle are the Bible (our *Power Manual*) and the Holy Spirit (our *Power Generator*).

Reading the Bible (Our Power Manual)

Most of us can describe a particular time when a Scripture seemed to inform and transform a potentially negative situation or the way in which we reacted to the situation. Studying and meditating on God's Word seemed to erase ungodly thoughts and beliefs from our minds. Words or thoughts that were once heated became civil; negative actions became positive ones. Hebrews 4:12 describes God's Word as "living and active, sharper than any two-edged sword" and "able to judge the thoughts and intentions of the heart." Few can withstand its power. We may not be able to control how others think, feel and behave, but we can control our own thoughts, feelings and behavior. First John 4:4 reminds us, "greater is he that is in you, than he that is in the world" (KJV). This means that we have the will and ability to react in a Christlike manner in various situations. The Bible promises this. As suggested by Paul in 1 Corinthians 9:24-27, it requires placing our minds and bodies under subjection—the kind of self-discipline that enables us to reject sinful thoughts and actions. But it can become easy to give up this ability when confronted with the many "isms" in society. Reading, meditating on and hearing God's Word will help us to be spiritually prepared to face prejudices in and around us.

Tapping Into the Holy Spirit (Our Power Generator)

When I was young, I thought Christians who spoke of being "convicted" by the Holy Spirit were strange. *What spirit?* I thought. *Were these people hearing voices? Seeing ghosts?* As I grew older and better understood the Trinity, I understood what they meant. Where would Christians be without the Holy Spirit? What would we do without the Comforter Christ promised in John 14:16, 26? Just when we seem to be at the end of our ropes and about to rely on our own means to handle a situation, the Holy Spirit provides insight—a spiritual nudge—to move us in the right direction. If you've ever been convicted that some thought or action was ungodly (or urged to perform godly ones, for that fact), that was the Holy Spirit at work. Because our wrestling match is spiritual in nature, we need a spiritual ally. You can also think of the Holy Spirit as our coach or trainer. Like a trainer, the Holy Spirit lets us know how to maneuver and what spiritual strategies to use to get Satan on the ropes, avoid societal pitfalls and to place God's interests above self-interests. When we follow the advice, victory is certain; when we fail to do so, defeat is imminent.

Let's take another look at the incident between my mother and her friend Tim. The episode could have become heated: her making racial remarks in reply to his remark; both of them spitting vicious comments and stereotypical statements at each other; the confrontation escalating until both were removed from the premises and possibly fired. But it didn't turn out that way; according to my mother, the Holy Spirit intervened. The Holy Spirit guided my mother to handle the situation differently. Tit for tat was not acceptable behavior. "An eye for and eye and a tooth for a tooth" would not serve God's purpose. The Holy Spirit enabled her to realize that although Tim had succumbed to temptation, she did not have to. And although Tim's negative comments about racial differences could have divided them forever, it did not. The Holy Spirit gave her the insight and ability to withstand Tim's verbal attack and to react in a Christlike manner.

Her behavior also provided a powerful example for Tim about what it means to be a Christian and a friend. But what about me? If you remember, I was angry enough to *physically* wrestle with Tim because of the unkind remarks he had made to my mother. Although I was not directly involved, I learned a valuable lesson as well. My mother's example in a potentially racially charged situation encouraged and inspired me to remember the dangers of prejudices and to rely more heavily on the Holy Spirit.

Think on These Things

We've all heard the saying "actions speak louder than words." Most people aren't impressed by what we say; they're impressed by what we do. Christians represent God. When we are confronted by temptation and do not succumb, it testifies that we are who we say we are. Have you ever watched parents at a child's piano recital? As their child plays, they beam with satisfaction and pride, not just because of the child's accomplishment but also because the child is representing them in a positive way. How would these same parents feel if, after hours of piano lessons and rehearsals, their child refuses to play, shreds the piano book in half and kicks the piano teacher in the shins—in front of the entire audience? Similarly, our beliefs, attitudes and actions can make God proud or ashamed. In this section, I challenge each reader to honestly reflect on his or her personal beliefs and behavior concerning prejudices. Many of the questions are broad such that you can begin to reflect on your general views, actions and experiences. More detailed issues will be raised in the next chapter.

1. Have you ever made comments or acted based on prejudices? When? Why? Did you realize that your comments or actions were prejudicial? How did you feel afterward? Did you reconcile with those involved? Why or why not? If reconciliation occurred, how did you feel afterward?
2. Do you know of prejudicial comments that have been made at your job? At home? How did you feel about this? What did you do or say?
3. Do you know of prejudicial actions that have taken place at your job? At home? How did you feel about this? What did you do or say?
4. Have you ever been a silent partner while prejudicial jokes (for example, racial, ethnic, sexual orientation, sex/gender) were made? What did you do or say?
5. Do you tend to blame certain groups for their condition or experiences (for example, the overweight for being overweight, the poor for their poverty)?
6. How would you feel if someone from a different race or ethnic group moved into the neighborhood in which you live? Next door?
7. How would you feel if a family member married someone outside of your race, ethnic group or class? If one of your children did?
8. Do you work closely with members of other races, religions, cultures or ethnic groups on a daily basis?
   a. Would you describe these relationships as positive or negative?
   b. Do you consider these coworkers your friends?
   c. In the last twelve months, how often have you gone to lunch with these coworkers?
   d. In the last twelve months, how often have you interacted with these coworkers outside of work (invited them to dinner, gone to their home for dinner, gone shopping or to the movies)?
9. When you meet people from diverse groups or cultures, do you *expect* them to think and behave in a certain way? Why or why not?
10. Do your children have multicultural toys, books, music and games?

Do you purposely buy multicultural music, toys, games or books for yourself and family?

11. How often have you or your family attended an event sponsored by a racial, ethnic or cultural group different from your own (for example, a bar mitzvah, gospel concert)?
12. Do you talk openly and honestly with your family about people who are physically different (for example, the elderly, physically challenged, obese, ethnic groups, racial groups)? What do you say?
13. Do you talk openly and honestly with your family about people who are mentally different (for example, the mentally challenged)? What do you say?
14. Are you comfortable interacting with gays and lesbians? Witnessing to them? Do you talk openly and honestly with your family about sexual orientation? What do you say?
15. Do you talk to your children about prejudices? Do you purposely strive to raise prejudice-free children? Do you prepare them for possible prejudices? Have you explained to your children that anyone can harbor prejudices or experience prejudices?
16. Do you praise and affirm differences and similarities in others? How?
17. Do you recognize and emphasize diversity found in God's creation? How?
18. What guidelines have you set to address prejudicial comments and actions that may occur within your family?
19. Are you honest with yourself and others about your own prejudices? How?
20. Do you avoid using blanket statements (for example, "those people" or "that group")?
21. Do you honestly and objectively discuss the prejudices and discrimination that have occurred in history (for example, the treatment of Native Americans, enslavement of people of African descent, the Holocaust, Japanese internment after Peal Harbor, Rwanda)?
22. Have prejudices ever influenced your political choices (for example, failure to consider or vote for a candidate largely because of sex,

race, ethnicity, sexual orientation)? How and why?

23. What Scriptures do you know that illustrate diversity and its importance? Do you rely on certain Scriptures to remind you about how to treat others? What are they?

What's Next?

Based on the types of prejudices examined here and some self-reflection, each reader is challenged to *honestly* identify a prejudice (or prejudices) that they harbor. Be like David in Psalm 139 and ask God to search you (a prejudice will probably be uncovered). What should you do now? Although you are thankful to God for making you aware of these feelings or behavior, you are stumped. What's next? You hadn't even *realized* your prejudices. And you don't want to unknowingly offend or hurt anyone again. You think, *Maybe it would be better to avoid the persons for whom you hold prejudices—at least until you conquer your prejudices. Better to be safe than sorry.* And can you somehow make it up to those you've offended? These are some of the types of concerns that may arise if you realize that you harbor prejudices. Awareness and acknowledging prejudices is the first step in addressing them. Answering the questions provided above can help you become more aware. However, avoidance behavior is not the answer. This approach only means that the persons or groups who have experienced prejudices because of us have been removed—not the prejudices themselves.

Even while working through our prejudices, God expects us to continue in ministry, no matter to whom. This means it may be necessary to witness to or interact with those we hold prejudices against. But if we reach out to those we are prejudiced against, isn't that being hypocritical? Satan would have us to believe this. By reaching out to others, regardless of our own shortcomings, we show God that we are obedient and that we desire to grow spiritually. Preparing ourselves to face these types of situations becomes less disconcerting when we realize that God is aware of our prejudices as well as our desire to change. God is also aware that Satan, society or self may tempt us to revert back to our old ways. Most importantly, God will not allow us to face a situation we cannot bear. When we realize this, we are more confident that we can handle possible prejudicial encounters. And one of the best ways to overcome prejudices is to interact closely with diverse groups to better understand commonalities.

But confidence alone will not bring victory. It will be necessary to rely on the Bible and the Holy Spirit. This means silently praying before we enter a possibly prejudicial situation or asking the Holy Spirit to enable us to handle it in a godly way (and knowing we have the ability to *choose* to reject Satan, societal pressures or our own self-interests). Meditating on Scripture and prayer also enable prejudicial thoughts to be removed from our minds. It may also mean asking God to bring memories or experiences to bear that *disprove* our prejudices. Sometimes it may mean removing ourselves from a situation if we feel negative attitudes and behavior beginning to flare up—there is nothing wrong with temporarily retreating from battle, regrouping and returning better prepared.

Facing our prejudices may also mean admitting them to others. Once, while traveling abroad, I was quite short with a bank teller. After being served, I apologized to her for my behavior. Initially she looked at me strangely, but smiled and graciously accepted my apology. Yes, I was representing America, but more importantly, I was representing God. It was important that my attitude and behavior reflect a Christian stance. Prejudices can be handled in a similar fashion. There's nothing wrong with apologizing to those we may have offended or admitting to someone, "I'm sorry for treating you that way, God is working some things out in my life." Not only will we feel better, but those involved will too. Saying we are Christians is easy. Living a Christian life is often challenging, especially when we forget about the spiritual warfare in which we are engaged. Relying on our Power Source and looking to the Power Manual can make identifying and doing away with prejudices a reality.

READ ABOUT

- **How Satan Works:** Luke 22:3-4; 1 Peter 5:8-9

FOR PEACE

For God is not a God of disorder but of peace.

1 Corinthians 14:33

Scripture notes, "all things should be done decently and in order" (1 Cor

14:40). From the beginning, God desired order. God took void—nothingness—and transformed it into paradise. Everything was perfect, tranquil and peaceful. But God's peaceful paradise was ruined—by sin. Similarly, when prejudices steal our peace, we are affected by the ungodliness of others, and the order in our lives is diminished. This is not God's design. God wants Christians to lead peaceful, productive lives. Those without peace can live chaotic, anxiety-filled lives; instead of thriving, they merely survive. Can you remember a particularly trying period in your life when you were without peace? Nothing seemed to go right. You may have been under attack by Satan. First Peter 5:8 describes him as a roaring lion, seeking someone to destroy. As far as you were concerned, he had gotten a whiff of your scent and was on your track, gaining with each passing moment. Or you may have been under attack by pressures in society. During that time, what kinds of emotions did you experience? Anxiety? Frustration? Depression? Fear? I would wager that it was difficult to exhibit the fruit of the Spirit.

When persons who harbor prejudices succumb to temptation, their attitudes or behavior can negatively affect recipients of prejudice. It can disrupt peace. And when people experience prejudices, they can lose peace and are less likely to be effective for Christ or in diverse interactions. It is difficult to have a healthy, productive life or actively engage in ministry with mixed-up minds, sagging spirits and heavy-laden souls. Just as bearers of prejudice must consider the possible influence of Satan, society and self on their prejudicial attitudes or behavior, recipients of prejudices can also be influenced by similar factors. For example, 1 John 3:8 reminds us, "the devil has been sinning from the beginning." This verse means that satanic forces have always and will always strive to undermine Christians and bring chaos to the human condition. Any method, including robbing persons of peace, is fair game. Similarly, studies show that all societies have historically condoned and continue to condone forms of inequality and discrimination and have accepted socially constructed hierarchies that esteem certain groups more than others. However, if you've experienced prejudices, you can have peace. Just as God can remove prejudices, God can erase their effects. In Matthew 21:22, Jesus encouraged us, "Whatever you ask for in prayer with faith you will receive." Mountains of anxiety, anger, fear, despair and indifference can be moved. But we must first *choose* to have peace and work toward that end. The Bible and the Holy Spirit are the means to help accomplish this goal.

Reading the Bible (Our Peace Manual)

Scripture reminds us of the many times persons were spiritually, physically and emotionally rescued when they called on God. Remember Lot in Sodom and Gomorrah? Shadrach, Meshach and Abednego? Daniel? Paul and Silas in jail? Jesus? We've all faced challenges, but few of us have been cornered by a dangerous mob. Or trapped in a fiery furnace. Or locked in a lion's den. Or shackled in jail. Or shipwrecked. Or hung on a cross. If God intervened throughout history to help people who were mistreated, alone or in danger, surely God will honor a request for peace. The Bible also describes the experiences of God's followers. Most were misunderstood, feared, hated and mistreated. Yet despite negative experiences, their spirits were often renewed when they tapped into God's power source to gain peace and continue in ministry. The Bible includes hundreds of Scriptures to minister to our specific needs. Have you ever read verses from Psalms and been renewed? Or energized by the relentless zeal of John the Baptist? Or uplifted by reading about Christ's love and compassion for humanity? Taking advantage of *all* that the Bible has to offer will help us to be victorious over the effects of prejudices.

Tapping In to Holy Spirit (Our Peace Generator)

Webster's Dictionary (1986) defines *comfort* "to strengthen, support, console in time of worry or trouble or to give hope." Interestingly, this same secular source also defines the word *Comforter* as the Holy Spirit. Even dictionary compilers recognize that the term *Comforter* can be equated with the Holy Spirit. What people do you look to for comfort, support and guidance during life's difficult moments? When faced with life's tough challenges, I often call my mother. I can always count on her for objective, honest advice or a kind, supportive word. Sometimes I contact my best friend, Monica. She is wise beyond her years. As a trained counselor, she can be counted on to give sound advice and a listening ear. Between the two of them, I am certain to get the help I need.

But sometimes when I call, my mother is not at home. And sometimes, I can only speak to Monica's voice on her answering machine. At other times, the situations are just too involved for them. God wants us to have competent Christian support, but people are limited. God wants us to rely on the Holy Spirit. But how often is the Holy Spirit our last source for comfort, guidance and support? How often do we fail to tap into this source of peace? Tapping into the *Peace Generator* can provide the guidance and support needed to stand against prejudices and to properly address them. The Holy Spirit will instruct us on what to say and how to react, even when others do not think or behave in kind. The Holy Spirit can also enable us to forgive others, rid ourselves of pain and find peace. And the Holy Spirit will provide the insight regarding how and when to combat prejudices.

Think on These Things

Have you experienced prejudices? In what way? As was requested in the first section of this chapter, each reader (especially those who have experienced prejudices) is challenged to consider the following questions. Honestly examine yourself to determine whether and how you've been affected by prejudices.

1. Have you ever experienced prejudices? When? How did you feel afterward? Did you reconcile with those involved? Why or why not? If reconciliation occurred, how did you feel afterward?
2. Is dealing with prejudices one of the primary sources of anxiety in your life? What type of prejudice(s) do you experience most often (based on race, sex, class, ethnicity, sexual orientation)? How do you address them?
3. Are you haunted by specific prejudicial experiences from your past? What are you doing to change this?
4. Do you feel uncomfortable or intimidated around other racial, ethnic or cultural groups? Which one(s)? Why? How do you deal with these feelings?
5. Do you blame, dislike or avoid entire groups because of past prejudicial experiences (e.g., all whites, blacks, Hispanics, women, men, the wealthy, the poor)?

6. Are there times when you "just don't want to be bothered" with people from certain groups? Which one(s)? Why?
7. Has exposure to prejudices affected your self-esteem? In what way? How have you dealt with this?
8. Have your experiences due to prejudices caused *you* to harbor prejudices? If so, what steps have you taken to remedy this?
9. Do you know of prejudicial comments and activities that have taken place at your job? At home? What did you do or say?
10. Do you become angry when thinking about prejudices in our society? How do you reconcile your thoughts and feelings?
11. How would you feel if someone from a different race or ethnic group moved into the neighborhood in which you live? Next door?
12. How would you feel if a family member married someone outside of your race, ethnic group or class? If one of your children did?
13. Have prejudicial experiences caused you to avoid relationships with coworkers of other races, cultures, religions or ethnic groups?
    a. How do you feel about these coworkers?
    b. In the last twelve months, how often have you gone to lunch with these coworkers?
    c. In the last twelve months, how often have you interacted with these coworkers outside of work (invited them to dinner, gone to their home for dinner, gone shopping or to the movies)?
14. When you meet people who are in some way different from you, do you *expect* them to think or behave toward you based on prejudices? If so, why or why not? During such encounters, are you generally proven correct?
15. Do you purposely strive to raise prejudice-free children? Prejudice-resilient children? Do you talk openly and honestly with your family about people who are different (for example, the elderly, physically challenged, obese, ethnic groups, racial groups, the mentally challenged)? What do you say?
16. Do you avoid using blanket statements (for example, "those people" or "that group")?

17. Do you talk to your children about prejudices? Do you prepare them to face possible prejudices? Have you explained to your children that anyone can harbor prejudices or experience prejudices?
18. Do you attempt to shelter or protect your children because of prejudicial experiences in your past?
19. Are you affiliated with an organization or group (for example, a church or community group) that provides support or counseling to address negative experiences such as prejudices? If so, have you taken advantage of this group?
20. If you are in pain because of prejudices, have you been able to minimize their outward effects (i.e., your comments and actions) for the sake of your family? Friends?
21. Are you honest with yourself and others about your fears, anxieties and frustrations because of prejudices?
22. Can you honestly and objectively discuss the prejudices and subsequent discrimination that have occurred in history (for example, the treatment of Native Americans, enslavement of people of African descent, the Holocaust, Rwanda)?
23. What Scriptures do you know that have helped you deal with prejudicial encounters? Do you rely on certain Scriptures to help you overcome possible negative side effects? To remind you about how to treat others? What are they?

It is difficult to face a painful past or deal with a peaceless present. Sometimes it seems easier to avoid negative emotions, even when they weigh us down. I remember when I first began to travel on business and my luggage was extremely heavy. It was tiring to carry several large suitcases, a purse and a briefcase through the many corridors of hotels and airports. As I traveled more often, I realized the need to pack light. I had to get rid of all that baggage. Several large suitcases became one large suitcase. Then one large suitcase became one small suitcase. Finally, one small suitcase became an overnight bag. I was able to travel more quickly and with fewer burdens when I rid myself of all that extra baggage. Is "baggage" from past prejudicial experiences weighing you down? Are mental, emotional and psychological suitcases hindering you? What are you going to do about it?

Just as reliance on the Bible and the Holy Spirit will enable persons to overcome prejudices for power, they will enable those who have experienced prejudicial treatment to find peace. It is important to acknowledge past prejudicial encounters, how they influenced you, your response (or lack of), and any negative outcomes from the experiences. Because of the nature of prejudices, it is rare to have a single occurrence in one's life. For example, racial prejudice and discrimination have been found to be a common part of the socialization process in the United States. However, intolerance is also declining (Gaertner and Dovidio 1986; Omi and Winant 1994). This means that members of minority groups will probably experience prejudicial episodes throughout their lifetime, but that prejudices can be combated and reduced. Attaining peace will thus require determination, faith and continued effort.

Given the possibility of confronting and combating prejudices, what can Christians do to turn the tide? How can the church respond? How *should* it respond? What are some of the thoughts and feelings congregants have about ways to address prejudices, specifically racism, stereotypes, discrimination and other "isms"? Several years ago, I performed an academic study to consider these issues. I posed questions to a group of 194 Christians—106 blacks and 88 whites—and examined their responses in general and based on race and race-sex differences. The respondents were members of two Baptist churches in the same community; one church was predominately black and the other predominately white. I selected the sites because although the churches were in close proximity (less than one block from each other), they seldom interacted. The findings were revealing and provide some insight into the strengths and challenges congregations may face if they endeavor to confront prejudices. Here is a summary of the findings.[1]

I compared and contrasted the attitudes and opinions of the Christians, followed by their suggestions for strategies to address prejudices and their related effects. Regardless of race (i.e., church membership),

---

[1]Readers should refer to appendix A and to S. Barnes (1997) for more sample details and quantitative results from the study.

most persons agreed that racism, discrimination and other "isms" continue to exist in society. However, *reasons* for the persistence of such social problems varied. Black respondents were more likely to attribute such problems to intolerance and fear, as well as the inability to combat racism and discrimination that occurs at a societal level. White respondents, on the other hand, believed that stereotypes, minorities blaming others for their negative experiences, and racial hostility were more valid contributing factors. However, both groups were in agreement that society is suffering from a lack of love and a lack of communication about the study topics. In general, blacks were more likely to associate continued interracial conflict with structural forces (i.e., macrolevel societal factors), while whites tended to attribute them to agency (i.e., individual or microlevel factors). As might be expected, these divergent views resulted in varied strategies and suggestions proposed by the two groups.

White respondents tended to make suggestions geared toward individual agency, rather than systemic change. And their suggestions tended to be more spiritually focused. For example, in order to address racism and help foster reconciliation, common responses by whites included showing more love, changing the hearts of persons and attempting to effect change within churches. In contrast, blacks tended to provide more practical suggestions that stressed establishing laws to check unequal treatment and developing educational programs for children to foster an appreciation of diversity. However, regardless of race and sex, respondents stressed sponsoring reconciliatory activities to increase awareness and prayer.

READ ABOUT

- **The Christian Assurance:** John 16:33
- **The Christian Legacy:** 1 Peter 2:9-12
- **How to Stop Satan:** James 4:7

Based on the overall results, persons from both congregations suggested that spiritual, practical and systemic transformations are needed to confront these types of prejudices and their effects. As I considered the findings from this study, several issues became increasingly clear: (1) despite varied backgrounds, heritages and experiences, it is possible for diverse groups to similarly identify pressing societal problems; (2) this same diversity may make it difficult to agree about *why* such problems exist and *what* strategies and solutions are needed to combat them; (3) a combination of macro- and microlevel solutions are necessary; and (4) continued (and honest) communication, education and interaction are central factors to start the process.

7

Making a Change

FOR POWER

For God all things are possible.

MATTHEW 19:26

People are often creatures of habit, and change can be difficult. The scholar Max Weber ([1921] 1978) wrote about the importance of charisma to energize and motivate group members. This trait seemed to be a particularly important factor in sustaining new religious groups. However, the author also noticed that in order to sustain the group long-term, charisma gradually became "routinized." The seemingly mysterious energy that originally compelled congregants, motivated them to challenge the status quo and moved them to even risk death for their cause was gradually replaced with formal rules and regulations, doctrine and hierarchy. Although the routinization of charisma is considered important for the long-term life of the group, it is often accompanied by the inability to foster change.[1] Weber's work illustrates the difficulty associated with affecting change once persons become set in their ways or fall into habitual ways of thinking and acting. Similarly, it may be difficult to make changes if prejudices are a part of our lives or if they are so subtle we have not been able to recognize them. This means taking a long, hard look at ourselves—based on biblical standards. Only by examining ourselves openly, honestly and continually can we uncover personal growth areas. This chapter focuses on specific strategies and suggestions to combat prejudices for power and peace.

[1]Refer to Roth and Wittich's (1978) edited work *Economy and Society* for Weber's assessment of power and leadership types.

Looking Inside

Have you ever made a comment or acted based on prejudices (for example, a racial or sexual slur, a negative thought about a poor person, avoidance of gays and lesbians or a disparaging comment about a full-figured person)? Chapter six focused on general issues relative to prejudices. This chapter may require a bit more self-reflection and specificity. Think objectively and honestly about *one* specific incident and answer the following questions:

1. What caused the comment or act? Was something said or done to trigger it? Were others directly involved or was this a result of secondhand information (something you heard, read or saw on television)? Did it occur in public or private?
2. Did you act based on that specific incident or did you act based on emotions from a similar, previous experience? Would you describe your response as an action or a reaction?
3. When and how did you realize that your thought or action was based on prejudice? How did you respond to this realization?
4. If others were involved, how did they act or react? Did you determine why they acted or reacted as they did?
5. Did the Holy Spirit convict you during or after your thought, comment or act? If so, how did you respond to the Holy Spirit?
6. Did you feel the need to talk to someone about the incident? If so, who? Is this person a Christian? Did you find his or her advice helpful? Was the advice biblically based? Did it make you feel better or worse?
7. Were you able to rely on Scripture during or after the incident? If so, what text did you find most helpful?
8. How do you think Jesus would have acted in your situation? Does Scripture mention Christ in a similar situation, or can a Scripture be applied to the situation?
9. In retrospect, how should you have handled the situation?
10. Did you learn anything from the experience that helped your personal Christian testimony? If so, what?

11. Were you able to forgive and forget (yourself and/or those involved)? How did you reconcile with the experience? If others were involved, were you able to reconcile with them or seek their forgiveness?
12. If faced with a similar situation in the future, how would you handle it?

After answering these questions, did you learn anything about prejudices? About yourself? Were you able to uncover the root of the incident? Was the exercise helpful in better understanding how and why you thought or behaved as you did? Here are some suggestions to deal with such situations in the future, reconcile past negative experiences and anticipate future positive ones. This will mean asking God for forgiveness, forgiving yourself and if possible locating and asking forgiveness from those you may have hurt or offended.

Change in Action

Someone might be thinking, *But how can I change? How can I alter prejudicial attitudes, beliefs and actions that have been a part of me for so long? That I wasn't even aware of?* Philippians 4:13 best answers these questions: "I can do all things through him who strengthens me." God (Power Source), the Holy Spirit (Power Generator), Jesus Christ (Power Line) and the Bible (Power Manual) are central in ridding ourselves of prejudicial attitudes and behavior. Here are twenty-five specific suggestions to help bring about change. Some of the suggestions and strategies are practical, some cultural and some are spiritual in nature. Some suggestions can be done alone, while others require a group effort. Some suggestions can be implemented immediately, while others reflect a process of growth and discovery. However, each will assist persons who harbor prejudices to overcome them for increased power in their lives.

Understand what it means to be prejudiced. It is easy to avoid the issue of prejudices and to continue to harbor them. Gain a clear understanding of the many facets of prejudices and their relationship to discrimination and "isms" (e.g., racism, sexism, ageism, classism). Many people incorrectly associate prejudices primarily with racism and with behavior (rather than also considering attitudes as well as the many ways prejudices can manifest themselves). Understand how the Bible describes and addresses prejudices (e.g., Gal 3:28-29; Num 12:1; Mt 22:39;

Song 1:1-6) and how situations can be handled from a biblical perspective. Try to understand how prejudicial attitudes, comments and actions are perceived from the point of view of the recipient. For example, how would you feel if a woman moved her purse from view just as you sat down beside her? How would you feel if you were called "honey" or "sweetie" at the workplace? How would you feel if a joke was made about your culture or heritage?

Use biblical standards. As noted in earlier chapters, identifying and addressing prejudices as well as acknowledging or appreciating diversity does not require Christians to automatically accept the attitudes, behavior and cultural dictates of others. We are challenged to examine and evaluate group differences based on biblical principles to determine how we should respond to them. Expanding our horizons will enable to us learn more about other persons and groups—the overall goal is increased understanding and awareness. However, if the other's beliefs and behavior run counter to those provided in the Bible, such beliefs and behavior (but not the inherent value of the persons or groups) should be rejected (Mt 10:16).

Admit that you have prejudices. Some people may refuse to admit their prejudices for fear of showing frailties. Others may present themselves as Christians who have never been prejudiced. Be honest. Don't be afraid to be vulnerable. Most of us have dealt with or are dealing with prejudices (whether we admit it or not). Also remind those close to you that you are not perfect, only striving daily to be more like Christ (Rom 3:23; 1 Jn 1:10; Ps 34:14).

Set personal and family guidelines. Make change a priority. Decide for yourself and with your family that prejudicial comments and actions are unacceptable. Establish clear consequences for inappropriate remarks and behavior, both personally as well as for family members and friends with whom you interact. Then give praise and positive reinforcement for godly attitudes and actions. If prejudicial ones arise, provide direct yet loving instruction and, for children, appropriate admonishing. Explain your standard and its importance to those close to you. Help your family and friends understand that prejudicial attitudes and behavior are ungodly and have detrimental effects for themselves and others. Live by the same standard as well. Be willing, if necessary, to separate from persons who try to undermine your goals (Josh 24:15; Ps 25:4-5).

Bounce back from setbacks. Try not to put yourself down if prejudicial thoughts and behavior persist. Ask God for the power to eliminate them. Relish personal victories, no matter how small (Hab 3:19; Ps 46:1; 28:7; 19:4; 18:2).

Believe that you can change. Reject prejudicial thoughts, beliefs and actions when they occur (Mt 17:14-20).

Realize that real change takes time. Most people learn prejudices over time. Ridding ourselves of them will also take time. Don't berate yourself if it seems difficult to change. However, be careful not to use this as an excuse for failing to make a sincere effort (Mt 19:26).

Remember the Golden Rule. Ask yourself, "Would I want others to act or react toward me based on prejudices?" or "Would I want others to evaluate me prejudicially?" (Gal 6:10, 13-14).

Make purchases purposefully. Buy multicultural books, magazines, movies and music. This should also include female and male dolls as well as racially and ethnically diverse toys, movies and music for your children. Exposure to diversity via as many mediums as possible will go a long way in helping to appreciate the richness of others (Gen 1:27, 31).

Target teenagers. Many teens are particularly vulnerable. During this period when they are "finding" themselves as well as trying to resist peer pressure, they are more susceptible to membership in hate groups.[2] Not only can they and others be hurt, but this will undermine the prejudice-free guidelines you have established for your family. Openly discuss prejudices as you spend quality time together. Dinner time, family walks or after church services are ideal times to get their opinions and share yours (Deut 6:4-7).

Praise differences and similarities. Learn to appreciate similarities *and* differences between sexes, among races/ethnicities and religious groups. Focus on a person's character rather than physical appearance or other distinguishing traits. Imagine how life would be as a member of a minority group. Read as much as possible about people from diverse backgrounds. Attend ethnic festivals in your city; taste foods, watch the dance presentations, listen to music. This will help fos-

---

[2]Research shows the increase in hate groups recruiting teenagers via the Internet.

ter a greater sense of appreciation for commonalities and diversity (Gen 1:27, 31; Acts 10:34-35; Eph 4:16; Col 2:18-19).

Minimize inaccurate and negative media influence. Honestly assess the media's portrayal of diverse groups. Determine the types of messages that are presented via television, radio, books and magazines that help foster prejudices (for example, portrayal of women and minority groups, images of physical beauty). Discuss these issues with your children. Assess how affected you have been by the media and in what ways (Rom 12:2; 1 Cor 1:20; 2:4-5; 1 Jn 2:15-17).

Identify possible prejudices in others. Reflect on prejudicial actions or comments to which you have been exposed (from relatives, family friends, associates and strangers). Be ready to address some often complicated and painful questions as you reevaluate your relationships and expectations from those who interact with you. This will help to better understand the complexity of prejudices. Don't expect to have all the answers. Be prepared for possible negative reactions from family or friends who may not understand the lifestyle you have chosen (for example, some may consider you "overly sensitive" if you refuse to laugh at "fat jokes"). Also help your children appreciate the "prejudice-free" lifestyle your family has embraced as well as understand that others may choose another lifestyle (1 Jn 4:5-9, 20-21).

Avoid making general statements. Sweeping generalities are very easy to make—and rarely true. Avoid making assumptions and judgments about a group based on one or a few experiences or observations based on a few members of a group. This will help you learn to appreciate others as individuals and to make decisions based on godly standards (Acts 10:9-48).

Expand your horizons. Do you interact with persons outside your race or culture? Do you have friends of other nationalities? How often have *you* invited a family of a different faith over for dinner? Fostering genuine, nontraditional relationships can go a long way in overcoming prejudices and also improve and expand your circle of friends or acquaintances. Also attend multicultural events—a bar mitzvah or an African American gospel music concert—to catch a glimpse of how others experience and celebrate life (Acts 10:28).

Understand history. Learn about the values and contributions made by those of different races, ethnicities, creeds, national origins, colors and religions. Explain the singular place in history of Mother Teresa. Discuss the contributions of Dr. Daniel Hale. How did Nelson Mandela help reshape the recent history of a nation? César Chávez? In-depth exposure to history can foster a deeper respect for diverse groups. Also learn about the experiences of Native Americans, the long-term effects of slavery and the Holocaust, and other historical epochs when prejudices were most evident. These may be emotional experiences, but they will also serve to sensitize you about how prejudices hurt. Choose reading material and films carefully; some authors and filmmakers encourage rather than dispel prejudices or minimize their existence (Hos 4:6).

Listen to your inner fears and concerns. New and different experiences can be frightening. Be willing and prepared to discuss your feelings and concerns. If you've had experiences based on prejudices, talking about them openly (and as soon as possible after the incidents) can help prevent you from harboring prejudices. Refer to suggestions later in this book on seeking counsel for ideas about appropriate outlets for counseling (Ps 23; Lk 8:15).

Remember that God created and loves us all. Scripture is full of examples of God's love for humanity and God's rejection of ungodly attitudes and behavior—including those due to prejudices. Read these types of Scriptures. Discuss them with your family during family Bible study. Talk about the sacrifice of Christ as God's ultimate example of God's love for everyone. Use the life of Christ as the perfect model of how we should treat others. Rely on Scriptures that illustrate the depth of God's love for humanity. There is an old saying: a person who thinks too much of himself thinks too little of God. This statement reminds us of the wisdom and power of God clearly evident in creation. These truths can reinforce the intrinsic value of others and strengthen a prejudice-free lifestyle (Gen 1:26-28; Jn 3:16; 2 Pet 3:9).

Learn something new every day. Expand your knowledge base. Educate yourself about others. Become more informed about the many ways society and the world reflect diversity. Research types of prejudice and approaches to take to combat them. The library is an excellent source of information. Refer to the appendix for a list of books and films that may be helpful (Is 1:17; Hos 4:6; 1 Cor 4:6-7).

Seek counsel. Do you have a friend with whom you can talk? A pastor? A particularly wise professor or counselor? Can they be trusted to give objective, sound advice? Are they nonjudgmental and discreet? Having someone to confide in who can give good advice or lend a listening ear will help during times when you feel overcome by prejudices. Choose your confidant wisely. The ideal choice would be someone who is knowledgeable about prejudices and their negative effects or who has overcome prejudices. If you don't know such a person, seek out a trusted, wise person with some experience in counseling or conflict management (Deut 5:1; Is 1:17).

Help yourself by helping others. Volunteer at a shelter, half-way home, inner-city center, weight loss facility, special needs clinic or AIDS hospice. Lend a helping hand in places that help people whose differences often cause them to be misunderstood, mistreated or ignored. This will help sensitize you to a variety of life experiences faced by others (Mt 25:31-45).

Put change in action. Ridding ourselves of personal prejudices is necessary, but prejudices on a societal level must also be addressed. Tap into economic, political and religious arenas to help bring about change. Concerned about how an ethnic group is portrayed in a magazine ad or television commercial? Women's ads? Contact and write the magazine or television station's public relations department. Seek collective support through your church or a community group. Be sure to follow up on your correspondence if the organization or establishment does not respond. Don't underestimate your influence or that of a unified group of people. Remember the academic study I described in chapter six? Although the community meeting that was held to discuss the results was, at times, tense, it created the desire on the part of the pastors and leaders from both churches to be proactive about interactions between the two congregations. Similarly, you can have great impact in your community and in society (Prov 31:8-9; Jn 21:14-17; Jas 2:1-9; 1 Jn 3:17-18).

Work to expose prejudices. One of the most interesting findings from my congregational study was the tendency for black and white respondents to view certain images differently. For example, blacks were more likely to associate certain colors with images they believed could result in negative views about race; whites did not consider these colors problematic. Were blacks *too sensitive?* Whites not sensitive *enough?* The answer is unclear, but the observation suggests the need to be discerning and to strive for objectivity and an open mind when considering issues like prejudices. Learn to examine society with a keener eye. Learn to identify subtle prejudices in and around you. Try to see life through the eyes of other groups—this will help to reveal prejudices that you may not have recognized before (1 Kings 3:9; Ezek 44:23; Heb 5:12-14).

Create a support or advocacy group. There's strength in numbers. Start a "Living Prejudice-Free" support or advocacy group in your church or neighborhood. Meet regularly to discuss personal challenges and success stories. Bring in speakers versed in topics such as reconciliation and conflict management. Distribute literature that will help the group live its motto. Refer to the appendix for ideas on organizing such a group (Acts 2:42-47).

Anticipate change. Get excited about your new outlook. Look forward to God's increased power in your life and ministry. Consider each day an opportunity to better appreciate and understand others (Mt 7:7-8).

Affirm your own uniqueness. Remember that you are fearfully and wonderfully made. Understand that it is possible to esteem oneself without feeling superior. Remember that you are special to God and were created for a specific purpose. When you feel better about yourself, you tend to think and behave more positively toward others (Ps 139:14).

I once read that the average person uses ten percent of his (or her) brainpower and that if eleven percent were used he or she would be a genius. Just think—one more percent could make that much difference. Now for a moment, reflect on your spiritual, personal and professional life. Now imagine the possibilities given just a *little* more power. Relying on God (the Power Source), emulating Jesus Christ (the Power Line), tapping into the Power Generator (the Holy Spirit) and studying the Power Manual (the Bible) will enable us to identify and overcome prejudicial attitudes and behavior. The aforementioned strategies suggest that the challenge to address prejudices is not a theoretical one, but is firmly rooted and grounded in the ability to change everyday thoughts and actions.

FOR PEACE

For God all things are possible.

MATTHEW 19:26

Someone who has been affected by prejudice might be thinking, *But how can I change? Yes, I'm carrying negative baggage, but what can I do? How can I forget the pain and hurt? Can I trust* them *again? Do I really want to?* Once hurt, it can be scary to expose ourselves to potentially hurtful situations again. But change is necessary to be whole. The word *holistic* has become a buzzword in many Christian circles. Everyone seems to be using the term, but some people may not really know its meaning and implications. Holistic Christian living involves loving and respecting God, others and self, despite our circumstances and experiences (Nouwen 1989; Dash, Jackson and Rasor 1997). When we experience prejudices, we may wonder, *God, why did you allow that to happen to me?* or *God, why are you allowing me to be hurt so much?* or *It's not fair, some people can say and do anything to others and never suffer the consequences.* If this happens, our relationship with God can become strained. And these emotions make it difficult to establish and sustain relationships with others.

Looking Inside

Have you ever experienced prejudices? How did you respond, act or react? Think objectively and honestly about *one* specific incident and answer the following questions:

1. What happened? Do you know what was said or done to trigger the comment or act? Were others involved? Were you physically harmed?
2. What were your initial emotions? Had you had similar experiences in the past? Did previous experiences influence how you dealt with this particular incident? How and why?
3. How did you respond? Why?
4. If others were involved, how did they act? Could you determine why they acted as they did?
5. Were you convicted by the Holy Spirit during or after your experience to think or behave in a certain way? If so, how did you respond to the Holy Spirit?

6. Did you feel the need to talk to someone about the incident? If so, whom? Is this person a Christian? Did you find his or her advice helpful? Was the advice biblically based? Did it make you feel better or worse?
7. Were you able to rely on Scripture during or after the incident? If so, what text did you find most helpful?
8. How do you think Jesus would have acted in your situation? Does Scripture mention Christ in a similar situation or can a Scripture be applied to the situation?
9. In retrospect, were you pleased with your response to the situation? Why or why not?
10. Did you learn anything from the experience that helped your personal Christian testimony? If so, what?
11. Were you able to forgive and forget (those involved)? How did you reconcile with the experience? If others were involved, were you able to forgive them?
12. Have you ever had an experience you believed to be prejudicially based, only to later learn that other factors were the cause? How did you feel afterward? Why?
13. If faced with a similar situation in the future, how would you handle it?

Dealing with the prejudices of others can be quite painful. We often don't understand why such episodes take place. Although most experiences do not involve physical harm, they can result in emotional and psychological scarring, loss of dignity, loss of trust in others and the belief that our feelings and experiences are unimportant. McCullough, Sandage and Worthington (1997) provide this suggestion for those who have been hurt: "If you want to regain the sense that your actions make a difference, forgive those who have, through hurting you, told you that you do not make a difference" (p. 201).

Change in Action

We can't force others to change, but we can change how they affect us. And sometimes our responses to life situations *can* subsequently alter the attitudes and behavior of others. Here are twenty-five suggestions to help during the healing process.

Understand what it means to be prejudiced. If you have been or are affected by prejudices, it is important to understand their many dimensions. What makes another person have a superior attitude? Or have preconceived notions about others? Or think and behave because of stereotypes? How have prejudices been manifested in society in the past? How do they appear now? What forms can they take? Where do they appear to be most prevalent? What arenas and groups in society are most affected? Many sociological and psychological studies have been performed on the subjects of prejudice, discrimination and the "isms" (note the references at the end of this book). Learning more about the factors associated with, the forms of and the effects of prejudices will help you better understand their potentially negative influences in your life and in the lives of others (Prov 3:13; 4:5-7; 11:12).

Admit hurt. Don't deny past negative experiences. Sometimes society hides or diminishes prejudices and their effects. Some believe that if we don't acknowledge a problem, it doesn't exist. Or maybe it will go away on its own. But this means no one has to change. Reject this mentality. When we fail to acknowledge and discuss our pain, we cannot find peace or remedies. Acknowledging the pain is the first step toward healing (Ps 55:16-18; Jas 4:10; Mt 11:28-30).

Know when to act and when to wait. Pray for a spirit of discernment. As Christians, God is always acting in our lives—leading, guiding and directing us—even when we don't realize it. Sometimes God works through us, other times God influences us through others. It is important to recognize when God wants us to act and when God says to us, "stand firm, and see the deliverance that the LORD will accomplish" (Ex 14:13). Sometimes we remain in negative situations or environments that drain our peace when God has instructed us to act—and provided a means of rescue. Each day, pain replaces peace as we sit and wait . . . and wait . . . and wait. And all along, God is waiting for us to act. We should not allow ourselves to be doormats for others. This is unhealthy for us and indirectly serves to justify prejudices in the minds of those who harbor them. Through God's guidance, we can know how to address prejudicial situations in a godly manner (Prov 3:5-6; 1 Pet 3:12).

Set personal and family guidelines. Decide that with God's help you will rid yourself of baggage associated with prejudices. Resolve to find peace. Decide *not* to do unto others as they have done unto you. Make this decision a family effort. This is often easier said than done. But rising above negative experiences is a sign of spiritual growth and maturity. Choosing to live a productive, godly life is one of the best responses to prejudices (Josh 24:15; 1 Pet 1:22; 3:10-11).

Bounce back from setbacks. You thought you'd gotten rid of some baggage, only to find that it had merely been rearranged. The load had not gotten lighter, you just found a new way to carry it. If setbacks occur, reject Satan's attempts to undermine the healing process. Be encouraged and continue to move toward healing (Ps 31:1; Is 26:4; Lk 18:27; Jas 4:7).

Believe that God can heal you. Expect God to give you peace. Look forward to the Comforter's work in your life. Meditate on God's Word. Believe and have faith in God and yourself (Mt 17:20; Mk 9:23-27; 10:27; 11:22-23).

Realize that healing usually takes time. For most people, the negative effects of prejudices aren't the result of one experience. Your peace was possibly drained as a result of a series of prejudices experienced over a period of time. Continual sexist comments, racist remarks or insensitive actions compound the effects of prejudices. This means that gaining peace may also take time. There are no magic cures. As you begin to reconcile these experiences, you may feel worse before you feel better. But be assured that a rainbow lies behind every storm cloud (Mt 19:26; Rom 8:26).

Forgive. Vindication comes from God—and it's usually much more effective than anything we can say or do. Fighting against prejudices doesn't mean holding grudges and having an unforgiving spirit. Just as Christ did, we should hate sin but still show love to those who transgress against us. This strategy is discussed in more detail in the conclusion (Mt 18:21-35; Rom 12:17-19; Col 3:12-14).

Protect and prepare children. Children can sense anxiety and turmoil. When their parents or loved ones are upset, children may internalize these concerns,[3] and this can affect their peace. Older children may realize the source of our pain and pledge allegiance with *us* against

---

[3]Refer to research by psychologists Freud (1960, 1963); Piaget (1951); Kohlberg (1981) as well as studies by sociologists Mead (1962) and Cooley (1964) on childhood development.

them. Make sure that children around you are not drawn into pain caused by prejudices. When you feel that they are able to understand the topic of prejudices, speak to them openly and honestly. Teach them how to appropriately combat prejudices they may face in the future (Deut 11:19).

Remember the Golden Rule. "Do unto others as you'd have them do unto you." No matter how we've been treated, this rule applies. But do not misinterpret this rule as reasoning to purposely allow others to mistreat you (Gal 5:13-14; 6:10).

Praise differences and similarities. Remind yourself daily that despite what others may think about you or attempt to do to you, there are things that you have in common with them. Many differences can be found in humanity. Remembering this unique combination of commonality and diversity will help prevent you from internalizing a "those people" or "us versus them" mentality (Gen 1:31; 1 Cor 4:6-7).

Identify possible prejudices in others. Central to the healing process is realizing that you may face prejudices again in the future. Remember, gaining peace will enable *you* to address prejudices. It doesn't mean that prejudices will disappear[4] (Mt 24:9-12; Heb 13:6).

Avoid making general statements. I once heard it said that some good can be found in the worst people and some bad can be found in the best people. Prejudices are prevalent in society, but all people don't harbor them. Just as the Civil Rights Movement reflected a rainbow of supporters, many people reject prejudices. Avoid the tendency to group people based on your negative experiences, stereotypes or a few negative experiences you've had with a few members of a particular group (Prov 3:7; Jas 2:8).

Expand your horizons. Grow daily. Exposure to a variety of people will help make you aware of how others face life's problems. This will also enable you to realize that prejudices can affect many different types of people and for a variety of reasons. As you learn and experience some of the challenges and victories of others who face or have faced

---

[4]Furthermore, persons should be discerning in this regard because prejudices are varied and can be manifested in varied ways and it is possible to label certain attitudes and behavior incorrectly. For example, findings from my congregational study suggest raced-based prejudices among both black and white respondents. However, class-based prejudices were not evident.

prejudices, feelings of being "the only" will diminish (Is 1:17).

Understand history. Never forget past episodes of prejudices in our country's and world history (the plight of the Native Americans, slavery, the Holocaust, apartheid, Bosnia, Rwanda). Remember these facts, not as ammunition to attack others, but as a reminder of what prejudices and discrimination can accomplish. Always be mindful of the times when unchecked prejudices snowballed into discrimination and "isms." By remembering the negative, painful periods of our past, we can also help insure that these types of activities do not reoccur. Also remember people who have been able to address prejudices in positive, proactive ways (for example, Otto Frank, Frederick Douglas or a family friend), how they have done so and lived victoriously, despite the prejudices they have experienced (Ps 90:1-4; Eccles 3:15).

Seek counsel. Sometimes healing cannot occur without help. When I attended seminary, there was a chaplain/counselor with whom students (who were pastors, Christian educators and other religious leaders) could talk. Sometimes we all need someone with whom to talk. If it appears that you are unable to reconcile past prejudicial experiences, seek the counsel of a trained professional—possibly a counselor, chaplain or minister. Speak with your pastor or a church elder. Talking with someone who can provide competent, objective, discreet aid can be the nudge needed to move you down the road to peace[5] (Ex 18:19; Judg 18:5; Lk 11:9; Rom 15:1).

Help yourself by helping others. Get involved in community service or outreach. Volunteer at a shelter, hospital, children's center or nursing home. Attempt to refocus your attention from yourself and your problems. Work with others who, like yourself, are valiantly facing a variety of tough challenges. By helping them in their struggle for peace, you may find it as well (Is 41:6; Rom 15:1).

Put change in action. Don't be afraid to speak out against prejudices. Once while shopping in an exclusive store, I noticed a salesclerk shadowing me. Was it my imagination? No, she was actually following me around the store. Did she expect me to steal? I finally turned and simply

---

[5]For example, Racism and Bigotry Anonymous (RABA) offers a 12-step program to overcome the effects of racism. Contact this organization at 256 Farallones, San Francisco, CA 94112-2939, 415-587-4207.

stated, "Young lady, please don't follow me around the store. If I want something, I will buy it." My statement wasn't made out of anger, but based on confident observation. The stunned, ashamed look on her face confirmed my suspicions. Speak out. Become comfortable confronting prejudices in a godly way. Learn to voice and write your opinions. Also correspond with those who can effect change on a societal scale. Realize that you can influence people and the powers that be as well. Increased involvement to combat prejudices will not only strengthen you, but provide an example for others (Acts 4:13-22; Eph 3:12; Phil 2:20).

Work to expose societal prejudices. Help others realize how prejudices are manifested, how society in general views those who are somehow different and how "minorities" are embraced. Do political, religious, economic and social factors play a role in diminishing or fostering prejudices? If so, in what way(s)? What can be done to increase support for those institutions and groups that work toward diminishing prejudices? How can institutions and groups that tend to foster prejudices be combated? Taking an active role in finding solutions is another positive outgrowth of finding peace[6] (Jn 9:4; 1 Cor 3:13).

Be discerning. Although studies continue to show that prejudices exist in our society, every situation that *appears* to stem from prejudices may not. It is important to be able to distinguish between prejudices and attitudes and behavior precipitated by other factors (the latter incidents are motivated by different reasons and may have to be addressed differently). Exhibit godly wisdom (Mt 10:16).

Create a support or advocacy group. Society is in need of more peace. Start a "Living Peace-Filled" support or advocacy group in your church or neighborhood. Address issues of conflict management and resolution. Discuss meditation and methods to relieve stress and tensions. Solicit speakers knowledgeable about the effects of prejudices, discrimination and "isms." Provide literature on suggestions to find peace. Target areas and people most affected by prejudices. Refer to the appendix for ideas on how to start an advocacy group (Rom 12:18).

---

[6]As was suggested in my congregational study, change must occur among individuals as well as at a societal level. White respondents tended to suggest the former and blacks the latter. The latter process requires group effort, energy, time and patience, but historically has tended to be most effective.

Increase prayer time. Remember Hannah? In those days, a woman's worth was primarily based of her ability to give birth to male children. Barren women were considered flawed, inferior and unblessed. Hannah's barrenness caused her much shame and embarrassment. She was also teased by her husband's second wife, Peninnah. Her pain became unbearable. Hannah went to God in prayer. She asked God to remove her misery. And God did (you are encouraged to read the entire passage for details about Hannah's experiences). Just as God heard and answered Hannah's plea, God can do the same for you (1 Sam 1:1-18; Jas 5:16).

Anticipate change. Get excited about the forthcoming changes in your life. Look forward to God's transforming peace. Get ready to find spiritual, emotional and psychological uplift and healing. As the gospel song encourages, "don't wait till the battle is over, shout now!" (1 Sam 2:2; Ps 5:11; 18:48; 32:11; 34:17-22).

Find a safe haven. Find a place where you feel welcome, wanted, relaxed and at peace. Such a space (for example, church, your home, a sauna, a meditation room) can provide a sanctuary for periodic rejuvenation. If you don't have such a place of solitude, create one (Ps 4; Jn 14:27; Phil 4:7).

Affirm your own uniqueness. Remember who you are. God has given Christians great responsibility and an even greater legacy. The prejudices of others can make you feel bad about yourself. Their potential to diminish self-worth and self-esteem makes prejudices so devastating and deadly. During these periods remember, "God doesn't create junk" (1 Pet 2:9).

Peace *is* available. It *is* possible to overcome the effects of prejudicial experiences and find peace. God wants us to be spiritually whole. Galatians 5:22-23 reminds us of the spiritual characteristics needed for holistic Christian living, "the fruit of the Spirit is love, joy, peace, patience, kindness, generosity, faithfulness, gentleness, and self-control." As Christians, we strive to exemplify these godly qualities in thought, word and deed. But if we are without peace, our spiritual fruit basket is incomplete and we aren't whole. But because of our relationship with the Trinity, peace is within our grasp.

Conclusion

FROM PREJUDICE TO POWER AND PEACE

Power and peace—each is important in the lives of Christians. Whether we have experienced prejudices or have thought or acted based on prejudices or both, reconciliation is necessary—and possible. Harboring prejudices limits our God-given power; experiencing prejudices can limit peace. Both hinder effectiveness as Christians and undermine our general quality of life. How do we encourage the type of change that allows the two parties involved in a prejudicial encounter—the bearer and the recipient—to both begin to understand, relate to and ultimately appreciate each other? Although the previous chapter includes a separate set of strategies for each party, it is important to also consider several broader issues that will inform us about the nature of the relationship between those who experience prejudices and those who harbor them. In this concluding section, I address the subjects of transformation, communication and healing and forgiveness—all within the very real context of a secular society that, in all estimation, will continue to engender prejudices and differential treatment based on prejudices.[1]

Hopefully each reader realizes that Christians have access to power both when we uncover and overcome prejudices in our lives and when we face and address the negative consequences of prejudices in our

---

[1]With regard to the expectation that prejudices and their negative effects will continue to exist in society, Bobo and Hutchings refer to racism as a marker and note, "Feelings of racial alienation reflect the *accumulated* personal, familial, community, and collective experiences of racial differentiation, inequality, and discrimination" (1996, p. 956, emphasis mine). Also refer to research by Bell 1992; Feagin 1975, 1991; Schuman and Scott 1989.

lives. Just as spiritual power is crucial, *having peace is a position of power as well.* And just as those who have experienced prejudices need peace, those who harbor prejudices are required to now embrace what is referred to in *Kingdom Ethics* as "peacemaking initiatives" that involve becoming "pacifists against prejudices" as they alter their previous attitudes and behavior and view previously ignored or ill-treated groups in new, positive ways (Stassen and Gushee 2003). Both bearers and recipients of prejudices are also challenged to make peace with themselves (Bloomfield 1996). Bearers must acknowledge prior injustices, repent and seek forgiveness (ibid.).[2] The authors of *To Forgive Is Human* note that genuine forgiveness requires the offender to seek forgiveness from those who have been hurt and requires the offender to be willing to lose face by being honest about the experience. Likewise recipients must address fears and pain and seek emotional release.[3] Both parties must seek spiritual liberty and work to maintain their newly found positions of power and peace. They must also commit to effect change in others. The transformation that occurs inside each party will inevitably surface as praxis manifested both individually and collectively. However, the tendency to detach is a common coping mechanism for both bearers and recipients. Bearers of prejudices detach from the reality of their inappropriate attitudes and behavior, and recipients detach from the pain of their experiences. The resulting distance prohibits relationships.[4]

The type of change I'm suggesting is impossible without establishing and maintaining healthy modes of both intra- and intergroup communication. What takes place spiritually can be influenced by what occurs socially, ethically, morally, economically, politically and culturally. Most sociologists (myself included), recognize the influence society has on its members, and we influence society as well. Views and corresponding behavior that have historically served to justify ill treatment of certain

---

[2]Also refer to Jas 5:13-16, which reminds us that confession leads to restoration.

[3]Sittser (1994) suggests that healing wounds is expedited when we focus our attention on the needs of others. He recommends encouraging and comforting others and holds that remembering the experiences of early Christians who were innocently persecuted will help strengthen the resolve of persons who are being mistreated.

[4]Heb 13:3 instructs us to pray for those who are mistreated as if we ourselves were suffering. This type of prayer will help develop empathy for others and enable us to begin to view others the way we view ourselves.

groups by others stem from the ways in which we come to understand ourselves, each other and our relationships with others. Numerous studies suggest that there is at least a tacit understanding in society that certain prejudices are acceptable.[5] For example, studies show that when many European immigrants came to the United States they often lived in areas near African Americans, sent their children to the same schools, and dealt with similar economic problems. However, according to Gunnar Myrdal (1962) in *American Dilemma:* "Recent immigrants apparently sometimes feel an interesting solidarity with Negroes or, at any rate, lack the intense superiority feeling of the native Americans educated in race prejudice. But the development of prejudice against Negroes is usually one of their first lessons in Americanization" (293).[6]

Keener (1997) characterizes such tendencies that result in divisions among Christians as *selective piety.* As has been presented in this book, how we think about and treat differences is communicated in various ways; hence the need to alter the ways in which we communicate about diversity and its importance. Sharp (2002) and others refer to this process as "deconstruction," and it requires critically considering our previous attitudes and behavior, especially those that directly or indirectly result in continued exclusion of others from important arenas in society. Deconstruction also requires the development of common ways of sharing and communicating to foster genuine relationships.

Ephesians 4:29-32 challenges us to refrain from evil communication and interaction that grieves the Holy Spirit *and* to replace negative emotions and actions such as bitterness, wrath, anger, slander and wrangling with kindness, tenderness and forgiveness. Although the motivation for such negative attitudes and actions differ for recipients and bearers of prejudices, each is called to the same godly outcome. But communication and transformation can be difficult due to the tendency to *talk around* controversial subjects, ignore pressing social problems, blame others or remain silent.[7] Dialogue between recipients

---

[5]Sharp's (2002) focus on the social construction of race and racism in *No Partiality: The Idolatry of Race and the New Humanity* can be applied to other forms of oppression due to differences.

[6]For similar observations, refer to "Has Europe Come to America?" *Gary American,* October 12, 1945, p. 4.

[7]Keener 1991; Sharp 2002.

and bearers is all the more difficult because the former group may be somewhat more open to a conversation, while the latter (possibly believing such a discussion will not benefit them and be accusatory in nature) may ignore or even fail to understand the need.[8] But the conversation is important for each party—though for different reasons. Furthermore, it will be crucial to move beyond words that suggest tolerance, reconciliation and acceptance to the corresponding actions.[9] This "applied Christian love" means *choosing* to address prejudices for power and peace. Separate examinations of the subject by Bacote (1997) and J. Julius Scott (1997) suggest that even in the presence of the Holy Spirit, a Christian must make a conscious commitment toward reconciliation. Being compelled to action (i.e., external change) is an expected byproduct of internal growth.

Change will result in the inclusion of previously excluded persons and groups. Bearers of prejudices will begin to see others in a new light and treat them in healthy ways; recipients of prejudices will reconsider the tendency to negotiate life outside the purview of those they believe harbor prejudices. According to Deddo (1997), resisting the type of transformation that results in reconciliation and covenantal fellowship "is not just a violation of an abstract commandment; it is resistance to the essence of who we are and who God is" (p. 65). The quality of relationships must be considered as well. Moving from prejudices to power and peace will result in genuine relations that acknowledge and appreciate, rather than ignore differences. This challenge is made in *Loving Across Our Differences,* where Sittser (1994) suggests that greater appreciation for others will emerge as we are subject to, forbear, serve, comfort, encourage, pray for and forgive one another.

But combating prejudices for power or peace will not be possible without healing wounds and forgiveness. *To Forgive Is Human: How to Put Your Past in the Past* by McCullough, Sandage and Worthington (1997) is quite possibly one of the most comprehensive books I've

---

[8]Keener (1997) also speaks to this tendency among black and white evangelicals.

[9]Washington and Kehrein (1996) *Breaking Down Walls: A Model for Reconciliation in an Age of Racial Strife* and Perkins and Rice (2000) *More Than Equals: Racial Healing for the Sake of the Gospel.* Sittser (1994) suggests the need to admonish one another as a last resort to motivate others to appreciate diversity.

read on the subject of forgiveness. I refer readers to the actual book for details on forgiveness, but will mention several points here that are germane to the issue of prejudices. The authors argue that there are benefits of forgiveness for all involved. The benefits for victims easily come to mind, but the authors suggest that it can be personally draining to deny when we have offended others.[10] I recall a conversation with an older professor who said that one of the reasons some persons had difficulty historically acknowledging racism and sexism is that in a society characterized by success through personal achievement and hard work, it is much too painful to acknowledge that some of your important successes are the result of the exclusion of large numbers of other people from various arenas of societal competition. Rather than face the possible pain and take part in self-reflection, it is easier to ignore it. Forgiveness enables those involved to restore dignity and reestablish power for the disempowered (yes, *bearers* of prejudice lose power and those without peace do so as well). It also reminds those involved of the moral and ethical guidelines of interaction and helps establish intergroup empathy. McCullough, Sandage and Worthington (1997) conclude:

> Forgiveness restores our belief that there are good people in the world. Even though we have been hurt, that hurt does not generalize to all people. . . .
>
> Forgiveness can improve mental health, reduce psychological and physical symptoms, lead to a greater sense of personal power and lead to greater life satisfaction. Moreover, forgiveness can also help us reap spiritual benefits. Spiritual benefits include added meaning and value to our lives, and transcendence from the concerns of everyday life. (pp. 195, 202)

Genuine forgiveness also requires both parties to realize and acknowledge the *importance* of the strained (or nonexistent) relationship and the desire to establish a healthy one. However, an "other-oriented" lifestyle stands in direct contrast to the rugged individualism often fostered in society (term noted by McCullough, Sandage and Worthington 1997). This means that establishing genuine relationships requires challenging and changing long-standing cultural and social norms about ac-

---

[10]Also refer to work by Pennebaker, Hughes and O'Heeron (1987).

ceptable and unacceptable ways of treating others.[11] I believe that this continues to be the primary obstacle to effectively addressing social problems such as prejudices.

One of the end results of healing for bearers of prejudices will be additional power; once healed, recipients will find peace. Just as 2 Corinthians 1:3-6 reminds Christians how God comforts during tribulations, it also reminds us that our negative experiences can be used, in turn, to counsel and comfort others who are physically and emotionally hurting. Those who harbor or experience prejudices may be unaware of their brokenness. Persons who experience prejudices are called to forgive and to release resentment and the right to retaliate (Mt 18:22)[12] and be discerning about the scope of future relationships with offenders (Russell 2004). In addition, part of their healing process includes *refusing* to give up their peace in the future. The authors of *To Forgive Is Human* also suggest, "reconciliation depends on the offender renouncing his or her previous hurts, confessing those sins and taking steps to insure that such hurts are unlikely in the future" (McCullough, Sandage and Worthington 1997, p. 124). This means that bearers of prejudices must refuse to succumb to future instances when they can hurt others simply because society condones it.

Sociologists often study ways in which people are influenced by society. The socialization process suggests that most people think and behave in ways that have been influenced by *social forces that are historical, pervasive and far-reaching. This is the context in which we are challenged to address prejudices. Our response will require reliance on the transformative nature provided by God and recorded in Scripture, a transformative power that demonstrates in very real, tangible, practical ways that people can positively influence society and establish genuine relationships that value a diverse humanity.

---

[11]Ibid. Chapter fifteen provides commentary on healing between groups that can be applied here. Their suggestions include perceiving the regret, determining whether the offense is likely to recur, developing some standard for restitution, ceasing to judge the offender and developing plans for cooperative efforts that will continue to build trusting relationships. The reader is also encouraged to refer to Jesus' model in Mt 18:23-34 and the chapter on forgiveness in Sittser (1994) *Loving Across Our Differences*.

[12]The reader should also remember that forgiveness is a continual process.

Appendix A

SOME CHRISTIANS SPEAK ABOUT PREJUDICES: A SURVEY

What if a group of Christians were asked their feelings about prejudices, color, race, class and about their behavior? What do they think? What would they do to bring about reconciliation? What specific suggestions would they make? I asked these questions to a group of 194 Christians: 106 blacks and 88 whites. Survey participants included 50 white females, 38 white males, 82 black females and 24 black males. Most of the participants were from working- or middle-class backgrounds, and they worshiped at nearby churches (one predominately black and the other predominately white). Everyone was at least 18 years old. The results reflect 10 survey questions and 2 open-ended questions. Each person also provided his or her race, education, sex and age. Although I made reference to this study within this content of the book, additional quantitative and qualitative findings are provided here for readers interested in more academic information on the topic. Readers are also encouraged to complete the survey and compare their responses to those of the survey participants.

Survey

Below are some statements that you *may* or *may not* believe. To what degree do you personally agree or disagree with each statement? For each statement, please circle 1 for "strongly agree," 4 for "strongly disagree," or 2, 3 for other degrees of response. When reviewing the results, the higher the value, the more the group *disagreed* with the survey statement.

	Strongly Agree	Agree	Disagree	Strongly Disagree
1. Teaching people about other races will help reduce racism.	1	2	3	4
2. Anyone can be successful if they work hard enough and long enough.	1	2	3	4
3. Due to past discrimination, job quotas are sometimes needed.	1	2	3	4
4. People who are not directly affected by racism can do the most to fight it.	1	2	3	4
5. Society influences people, people don't influence society.	1	2	3	4
6. When I think of the word *white* it is usually negative.	1	2	3	4
7. All black or all white churches are no big deal; people worship God differently.	1	2	3	4
8. People tend to live where they feel safe.	1	2	3	4
9. Some images (e.g., bad guy wears black, white as snow) can influence a person's image of race.	1	2	3	4
10. Most government programs designed to help minorities end up hurting them.	1	2	3	4

General Comments:

1. What is the greatest problem facing this society in terms of race relations?
2. What can the church do to help address this problem?

Survey Results: Average Responses by Race

	Black	White
1. Teaching people about other races will help reduce racism.	1.61	1.87
2. Anyone can be successful if they work hard enough and long enough.	3.59	3.48
3. Due to past discrimination, job quotas are sometimes needed.	1.71	2.82*
4. People who are not directly affected by racism can do the most to fight it.	2.58	2.80*
5. Society influences people, people don't influence society.	3.32	2.99*
6. When I think of the word *white* it is usually negative.	3.07	3.33*
7. All black or all white churches are no big deal; people worship God differently.	3.05	3.22
8. People tend to live where they feel safe.	3.48	3.44
9. Some images (e.g., bad guy wears black, white as snow) can influence a person's image of race.	2.35	2.66*
10. Most government programs designed to help minorities end up hurting them.	3.43	3.36

Key: *Identifies group responses that are very different for a given question. The higher the value, the more the group disagreed with the statement.

Summary of Survey Results by Race:

Regardless of race (i.e., church congregation), group responses were similar for 5 of the 10 questions. Persons agree that increased teaching about races will improve relations (Q1) and tend to reject rugged individualism (Q2). Both groups also believe separate church and residential arrangements are influenced by factors other than diverse styles or safety, respectively (Q7, Q8) and that past government programs to aid minorities were not detrimental (Q10). However, disparate responses are evident when color symbolism is examined (Q6, Q9), and blacks tend to disagree more than whites with the survey statements. Whites were most likely to reject the use of quotas to address past discrimination (Q3). Lastly, groups are split on questions that consider the role of group action in society. Blacks more than whites tend to believe that efforts to address racism should be championed by those most directly affected (Q4), while whites believe individual agency is more effective at altering society than vice versa (Q5).

Survey Results: Average Responses by Race and Sex

	Black Male	Black Female	White Male	White Female
1. Teaching people about other races will help reduce racism.	1.54	1.63	1.86	1.88
2. Anyone can be successful if they work hard enough and long enough.	3.38	3.66	3.43	3.52
3. Due to past discrimination, job quotas are sometimes needed.	1.88	1.66	3.00	2.69*
4. People who are not directly affected by racism can do the most to fight it.	2.38	2.64	3.03	2.61*
5. Society influences people, people don't influence society.	3.05	3.40	2.94	3.02*
6. When I think of the word *white* it is usually negative.	3.13	3.05	3.24	3.40*
7. All black or all white churches are no big deal; people worship God differently.	2.88	3.10	3.31	3.16*
8. People tend to live where they feel safe.	3.50	3.48	3.55	3.36
9. Some images (e.g., bad guy wears black, white as snow) can influence a person's image of race.	2.46	2.32	2.59	2.71*
10. Most government programs designed to help minorities end up hurting them.	3.54	3.40	3.38	3.35

Key: *Identifies group responses that are very different for a given question. The higher the value, the more the group disagreed with the statement.

Summary of Survey Results by Race and Sex

Group differences are evident for 6 of the 10 questions. Similar to the results for race provided on the previous page, regardless of race or sex, respondents support the need for increased teaching to reduce racism (Q1). Furthermore, most respondents disagree with the questions that gauge rugged individualism (Q2), safety as the rational for residential patterns (Q8), and negative outcomes of minority-focused government programs (Q10). However, responses for the remaining questions are influenced by the intersection of the sex and race of the respondent. For example, white males are more likely than the three remaining groups to oppose the use of quotas to rectify past discrimination; black females are most supportive of such an approach (Q3). Black and white males have the most disparate views about which groups can be most influential in combating racism (Q4). In contrast, black females are more apt to support individual initiative over structural changes rather than the converse; white males have the lowest average response for this indicator (Q5). And although all four groups disagree with the association of the color *white* with negative connotations, white females have the highest average response (Q6). A similar pattern is evident for the final question on color images (Q9). Lastly, the response pattern for Q7 suggests that black males are the least likely to view racially segregated churches suspiciously. Survey findings suggest that when race and sex are considered together, the opinions, strategies and suggestions tend to be more varied than when race is considered alone. This general observation informs our understanding of the possible effects of *individual* diversity (i.e., a person's race, sex, class, sexual orientation, ethnicity, religion) on fostering appreciation of diversity across groups, understanding diverse experiences and finding solutions to address such social problems.

Interview Results: Comments and Suggestions

Note: Common intergroup responses are identified with an asterisk (*).

1. What is the greatest problem facing this society in terms of race relations?

Five Most Frequent Responses by Blacks:

Continued racism, discrimination, intolerance
Lack of love*
Lack of appreciation of group differences
Fear
Lack of communication*

Five Most Frequent Responses by Whites:

People blaming other people for their situations/experiences
Lack of love/trust/understanding*
Stereotypes
Racial hostility
Lack of communication*

2. What can Christians do to help this problem?

Five Most Frequent Responses by Blacks:

Increased awareness of other groups
Institute programs that foster racial interaction and reconciliation*
Pray*
Change laws to combat injustices
Teach/train children to appreciate others

Five Most Frequent Responses by Whites:

Show love
Institute programs that foster racial interaction and reconciliation*
Pray*
Bring about change via churches
Change our hearts

Summary of Findings

According to the quantitative and qualitative findings from the survey, regardless of race or sex, the groups acknowledge the existence of prejudices and racism. However, opinions differ in terms of how to work toward reconciliation. Racial groups have different opinions about how to correct past employment prejudices, discriminations and "isms." White respondents tend to focus on agency-based strategies (i.e., change for each person as an individual). Blacks tend to desire systemic changes (i.e., change in governmental policies and laws). Blacks and whites tend to have similar *views* about the study topics. However, the results show differences in how whites and blacks *act* or *would act* to remedy these problems.

Appendix B

HOW TO ORGANIZE A RECONCILIATION SUPPORT GROUP

Here are some suggestions for organizing a reconciliation or advocacy group in your community. Also contact local multicultural churches or the human rights commission in your state for advice and related information.

1. Start

Bring together a group of like-minded persons (i.e., persons with the same desire to help bring about reconciliation). Don't worry if the group is initially small. Be determined and get started.

2. Choose a Location

Choose a site that is central to the community. You want as many diverse people to have access to the group as possible. Find a community center or church that would be available. If a location within a diverse community cannot be found, find several locations that are central to those communities you wish to target for members and alternate meetings between the various areas.

3. Be Welcoming

To be most effective, the advocacy group should welcome all persons, regardless of race, color, ethnic background, creed, sexual orientation, gender or religion.

4. Involve Trained Persons

Involve persons with training in reconciliation or conflict management. Contact persons with backgrounds in group dynamics or counseling to get involved. These persons can provide invaluable information and suggestions or act as group facilitators. If such persons cannot be located, find group volunteers willing to take community classes or correspondence courses on the subjects of prejudice and "isms." (Note: the types of questions posed in chapters six and seven of this book may be helpful to spark discussion.)

5. Determine the Group's Mission

It will be important to determine a mission statement and goals. What will be the group's purpose? Will the group be informal? Will it be primarily a discussion group? Will it have economic and political dimensions? Be activist in nature? Answering these types of questions early on will provide guidance for the group and minimize floundering.

6. Determine Agendas

Set aside a certain portion of the gatherings to openly discuss issues related to prejudices and personal experiences of members and guests. Also spend time developing plans to bring about community awareness and involvement. Invite outside speakers. Show movies. Attend multicultural activities. Sometimes just spend time together and getting to know each other. Schedule a variety of creative activities that will inform, motivate and inspire change.

7. Inform the Community

Distribute fliers. Publicize at churches and neighborhood locations via the media. Spread the news by word of mouth. Notify and invite as many people as possible. Continue to keep the community informed about the group's progress. This may spark the interest of others within the area.

8. Evaluate the Program

Ask members and guests to evaluate the program's structure, goals, activities and effectiveness at the outset and at periodic intervals.

9. Learn from Others

Get involved as a group with local and national organizations that work for equality and civil rights. A few organizations are listed below:

American Civil Liberties Union (ACLU)
132 West 43rd Street
New York, NY 10036
212-944-9800

Anti-Defamation League (30 regional offices in the U.S.)
www.adl.org/adl.asp

Christian Community Development Association (CCDA)
www.ccda.org

Christians for Biblical Equality (CBE)
www.cbeinternational.org

National Institute Against Prejudice and Violence
712 West Lombard Street
Baltimore, MD 21201
410-706-5170

National Association for the Advancement of Colored People (NAACP)
4805 Mt. Hope Drive
Baltimore, MD 21215
410-358-8900

Racism and Bigotry Anonymous (RABA)
256 Farallones
San Francisco, CA 94112-2939
415-587-4207

Southern Christian Leadership Conference (SCLC)
334 Auburn Avenue NE
Atlanta, GA 30312
404-522-1420

Sojourners: Christians for Justice and Peace
2401 15th Street NW
Washington, DC 20009
phone: 202-328-8842
fax: 202-328-8757
sojourners@sojo.net
www.sojo.net

Appendix C

SUGGESTED READING AND FILMS FOR ADULTS

This list of books and films for adults provides insightful information on subjects germane to this book.

SIX BOOKS

On Reconciliation

Loving Across Our Differences, by Gerald Sittser (InterVarsity Press)

Raising the Rainbow Generation: Teaching Your Children to be Successful in a Multicultural Society, by Darlene and Derek Hopson (Fireside Books)

On Overcoming

Power Thoughts, by Robert Schuller (Harper)

Making Peace with Yourself, by H. Bloomfield (Ballantine Books)

To Increase General Knowledge and Awareness

Race Matters, by Cornel West (Beacon Press)

Prejudice, Discrimination, and Racism: Historical Trends and Contemporary Approaches, edited by J. F. Dovidio and S. L. Gaertner (Academic Press)

TEN FILMS

The specific theme for each film is provided in brackets. Many of the films listed for adults are also appropriate for older youth. The films followed by an asterisk should be reviewed by adults prior to showing them to youth.

Eye on the Prize (series) [black/white race relations, class, social action]
The Joy Luck Club [Asian experiences]
Gandhi [India, caste, humanitarian efforts for the poor and oppressed]
*Schindler's List** [Jewish experiences, Holocaust]
Corrina, Corrina [interracial relationships, class]
*Roots** (series) [black/white race relations, slavery, class, poverty, family]
Mask [physical differences]
Dances with Wolves [Native American/white relations]
On Golden Pond [age]
Whale Rider [gender, age]

Appendix D

SUGGESTED READING AND FILMS FOR CHILDREN

This list of books and films for children provides engaging, age-appropriate information on subjects germane to this book.

SIX BOOKS

To Increase General Knowledge and Awareness

33 Multicultural Tales to Tell, by Pleasant DeSpain (August House)

Tortillitas para Mama, by M. Griego, B. Bucks, S. Gilbert and L. Kimball (Henry Holt)

Lon Po Po: A Red-Riding Hood Story from China, by Ed Young (Putnam & Grosset Group)

On Overcoming

Designed by God, So I Must Be Special, by Bonnie Sose (Character Builders for Kids)

Roll of Thunder, Hear My Cry, by M. Taylor (Puffin Books)

On Physical Differences

About Handicaps: An Open Family Book for Parents and Children Together, by Sara Stein (Walker)

FIVE FILMS

The specific theme for each film is provided in brackets.

Sounder [black/white race relations, class, poverty]

The Diary of Anne Frank [Jewish experiences, Holocaust]

Pocahontas: Her True Story [Native American/white relations]

Nestor: The Long-Eared Christmas Donkey [physical differences]

Mulan [Asian experiences, gender]

Glossary of Primary Terms

affirmative action. Organized effort, in response to historic discrimination, to improve the educational and employment opportunities of qualified minority groups and women.
ageism. Discrimination based on age.
agency. Freewill; the ability to make choices.
androgynous. Taking on both masculine and feminine characteristics (attitudes and/or behavior); taking on, reversing or mixing traditionally male and female roles.
assimilate. To absorb one's culture/traditions into the culture/traditions of another group; to incorporate or convert such that one's previous culture/traditions are replaced by those of another group; *assimilate* differs from the term *integrate,* which reflects mixing one's culture/traditions with those of another group such that the central facets of the original culture/traditions remain intact.
aversive racism. Subtle form of racism that usually manifests in discomfort, uneasiness, disgust, fear and avoidance of minority groups; considered challenging to uncover because aversive racists may not be aware of their racist tendencies.
biracial. Persons with parents from two different racial categories (for example, Tom would be considered biracial if one parent is white and the other is black).
call-and-response tradition. A worship style endemic to the black church that reflects communication between worship leaders and congregants; emphasizes the importance and involvement of persons in the pews to take part in effective worship; includes requests by ministers during sermons for "Amen" when truth is being spoken and responses by congregants as well as the understood acceptance congregants have to verbally affirm statements, songs and other activities during service. Studies suggest that the process of communication and interaction during services can validate congregants, reinforce a sense of community within the church and provide persons with an environment where their "voices" can be raised and heard without reprisal.
change agents. Persons who are actively engaged in altering existing beliefs, norms and ideas as well as laws in order to address a social problem.

classism. Prejudice based on differences in economic status and other factors usually associated with economic status or social class such as educational attainment and wealth.

creed. Broadly defined as a person's set of basic beliefs that guide her/his life; creeds are often shaped by culture or religious beliefs and influence the attitudes and behavior of adherents.

cultural relativity. Acknowledging, understanding and appreciating cultural differences such as lifestyles, beliefs, customs, food, clothing, language, hairstyles (i.e., cultural markers) even though they may differ from one's own. An outlook also characterized by the desire and ability to objectively evaluate other cultures based on their specific cultural markers rather than based on one's own.

discernment. The ability to grasp or understand that which is obscure; insight; perception.

discrimination. Unequal treatment or favor based on factors other than individual merit; also referred to as prejudicial behavior.

disempower. To oppress; to take authority from.

diversity. Heterogeneity; variety; the condition of being different.

empower. To give authority to; to uplift; to enable.

ethnicity. Socially constructed term used to describe a person based on her/his connection to a given country or land mass; it also reflects diverse customs, lifestyles and beliefs; examples include German American (a person of German and American descent) or Italian American (a person of Italian and American descent).

ethnocentrism. Evaluating other groups or cultures based on our specific group or cultural criteria rather than based on their own; generally considered a more subjective process that often leads to devaluing the group under evaluation or being overly critical or negative about them.

female genital mutilation. Cultural practice in parts of Africa and Asia that usually involves removing portions or all of the female genitalia.

gender. Socially constructed term to characterize attitudes and behavior that manifest based on one's sex; reflects use of terms such as *man/woman, boy/girl;* for example, females are generally socialized to think and behave like "women" and males are socialized to think and behave like "men."

hierarchy. Ranking or classifying persons or groups based on some socially accepted criteria, usually based on economic or social standing. Hierarchies are also established based on perceived group ability, professions or access to power.

homogamy. The tendency to interact with, feel connected to or establish relationships with persons who have similar beliefs, interests and backgrounds; often used when describing romantic relationships.

homophobia. Irrational fear of homosexuality or homosexuals.

inequality. Disparity, usually a result of unequal treatment or unequal access to resources; disparity in opportunity or distribution of resources.

institutionalized discrimination. Process that leads to unequal treatment and/or outcomes based on the actions or activities of organized, structured institutions, groups and organizations in society; unequal treatment that has become codified.

interethnic. Dynamics that occur across ethnic groups.

intergroup. Dynamics that occur across groups; for example, interaction between females and males (i.e., intersex or across sexes), blacks and whites (i.e., interracial or across races) or the middle class and working class (i.e., interclass or across economic classes).

interracial. Dynamics that occur across racial groups.

intraethnic. Dynamics that occur within a specific ethnic group.

intragroup. Dynamics that occur within a specific group; for example, interaction among working class and middle class African Americans (i.e., intraethnic or within ethnicity), Asian and Cuban women (i.e., intragender or within gender) or freshmen and sophomores (i.e., intracollegiate or within college classifications).

intraracial. Dynamics that occur within a specific racial group.

majority group. Group of persons that usually numerically outnumber other groups of persons; also refers to a group that has historically been in a position of economic, social and political power over other groups.

minority group. Group of persons that are usually numerically underrepresented as compared to other groups of persons; usually also refers to a group that has historically lacked economic, social and political power as compared to the majority group.

multiethnic. Many ethnicities; term used to characterize persons, groups or dynamics that are mixed in terms of ethnicity.

multiracial. Many races; term used to characterize mixed-raced persons, groups or dynamics.

oppression. Unjust exercise of authority or power over another person or group; a sense of being weighed down in body, mind or spirit.

peace. The ability that comes from God that enables Christians to reject disturbing, disquieting or upsetting thoughts or behavior that can result from negative experiences; the ability to live in a state of relative spiritual calm despite emotionally and psychologically negative experiences.

poverty. Lacking the socially acceptable amount of economic or material resources. In the United States, poverty is assessed based on a socially constructed threshold calculated by estimating minimal expenses for subsistence.

power. The ability that comes from God that enables Christians to think, feel and behave in godly ways that parallel those of the life of Jesus Christ; it reflects the desire to choose to make decisions (thoughts and deeds) that are pleasing to God.

prejudice. Rigid, irrational, inaccurate beliefs or attitudes about others based largely on a faulty assessment of oneself and others; prejudging others, usually in a negative fashion, even in the face of contradictory information or with little regard to facts.

race. Socially constructed term historically used to categorized people that have biologically transmitted traits in common (e.g., skin color, hair texture, facial features); historically, a three-part typology included Caucasoid, Negroid and Mongoloid; historically used for descriptive purposes, but now often used to suggest and reflect social status and inequality.

racial reconciliation. To establish genuine interactions and relationships across racial groups; a process typically fostered by education and interaction.

racism. Discrimination based on race.

rugged individualism. Belief that each person is largely responsible for his/her own destiny; ideology that emphasizes personal responsibility and hard work to achieve desired outcomes.

self-reflection. The ability to thoughtfully and objectively examine one's own attitudes and/or behavior usually to determine strengths and growth areas; reflects a continual process.

sex. Socially constructed term to distinguish between females and males; historically used when considering biological differences (e.g., size, weight, reproductive processes, pain thresholds) between the two groups; historically used for descriptive purposes, but now often used to suggest and reflect social status and inequality.

sexism. Discrimination based on whether one is female or male; can also be defined as discrimination based on gender (woman, man, boy, girl).

socialize (socialization). The lifelong process by which persons come to realize and understand themselves, their culture and their surroundings; generally includes various forms of communication and interaction over the life course.

socially constructed. Created in society, generally based on the influences of a group in power; suggests variability across societies, cultures and groups.

stereotype. An exaggerated generalization applied to every person in a group; usually reflects an oversimplification or biased judgment.

structural forces (systemic forces, social forces). Macrolevel organizations, institutions and ideologies that affect and influence persons at the microlevel; examples include the government, the economic system (capitalism, communism, socialism), the legal system, religion, the media, the ideology of the family, racism, sexism and classism.

working poor. Persons who are employed, but whose annual income is below the official poverty threshold.

xenophobia. Fear and hatred of foreigners or strangers or things considered foreign or strange.

Bibliography

Adorno, Theodore, Elsie Frenkel-Brunswik, Daniel J. Levinson and R. Nevitt Sanford. 1950. *The authoritarian personality*. New York: Harper & Brothers.

Aldridge, Deloris. 1989. Interracial marriage: Empirical and theoretical considerations. In *Black male-female relationships,* ed. Deloris Aldridge, pp. 17-34. Dubuque: Kendall/Hunt.

Anderson, Elijah. 1997. *Streetwise: Race, class, and change in an urban community*. Chicago: University of Chicago Press.

Apostle, Richard, Charles Glock, Tom Piazza and Marijean Suelzle. 1983. *The anatomy of racial attitudes*. Berkeley and Los Angeles: University of California Press.

Arvanites, T. M., and M. A. Asher. 1998. State and country incarceration rates: The direct and indirect effects of race and inequality. *American Journal of Economics and Sociology* 57 (2): 207-21.

Bacote, Vincent. 1997. Theological method in black and white. In *The gospel in black & white: Theological resources for racial reconciliation,* edited by Dennis L. Okholm, pp. 49-57. Downers Grove, IL: InterVarsity Press.

Barnes, Harry E. 1972. *Pearl Harbor after a quarter of a century*. New York: Arno Press.

Barnes, Sandra. 1997. Practicing what you preach: An analysis of racial attitudes of two Christian churches. *Western Journal of Black Studies* 21 (1): 1-11.

———. 2005. *The cost of being poor: A comparative study of life in poor urban neighborhoods in Gary, Indiana*. New York: State University Press.

———. Forthcoming. Whosoever will let *her* come: Gender inclusivity in the black church. *Journal for the Scientific Study of Religion*.

Barnes, Sandra, and Charles Jaret. 2003. The "American dream" in poor urban neighborhoods: An analysis of home ownership attitudes and behavior and saving. *Sociological Focus* 36 (3): 219-39.

Bell, Derrick. 1992. *Faces at the bottom of the well*. New York: Basic Books.

Bem, Sandra. 1981. Gender schema theory: A cognitive account of sex-typing. *Psychological Review* 88 (4): 354-64.

———. 1993. *The lenses of gender: Transforming the debate on sexual inequality*. New Haven, CT: Yale University Press.

Bengston, Vern, Garardo Marti and Robert Roberts. 1991. Age-group relationships: generational equity and inequity. In *Parent-child relations throughout the life,* edited by Karl Pillemer and Kathleen McCartney, pp. 253-78. Hillsdale, NJ: Lawrence Erlbaum Associates.

Billingsley, Andrew. 1992. *Climbing Jacob's ladder: The enduring legacy of African- American families.* New York: Touchstone.

Blau, P., and O. Duncan. 1966. Some preliminary findings on social stratification in the United States. *ACTA Sociologica* 9 (1-2): 4-24.

Bloomfield, Harold. 1996. *Making peace with yourself.* New York: Ballantine.

Blumer, Herbert. 1958. Race prejudice as a sense of group position. *Pacific Sociological Review* 1:3-7.

Bobo, Lawrence. 1988. Group conflict, prejudice, and the paradox of contemporary racial attitudes. In *Eliminating racism: Profiles in controversy,* edited by P. A. Katz and D. A. Taylor, pp. 85-114. New York: Plenum.

Bobo, Lawrence, and Vincent Hutchings. 1996. Perceptions of racial competition: Extending Blumer's theory of group position to a multiracial social context. *American Sociological Review* 61:951-72.

Bonilla-Santiago, G. 1992. *Breaking ground and barriers: Hispanic women developing effective leadership.* San Diego: Marin Publications.

Boswell, Terry. 1986. A split labor market analysis of discrimination against Chinese immigrants, 1980-1992. *American Sociological Review* 51 (3): 352-71.

Briscoe, Stuart. 1984. *The fruit of the Spirit: Growing in Christian character.* Colorado Springs: WaterBrook.

Brown, Irene. 1997. Explaining the black-white gap in labor force participation among women heading households. *American Sociological Review* 62:236-52.

Brownsberger, W. N. 2000. Race matters: Disproportionality of incarceration for drug dealing in Massachusetts. *Journal of Drug Issues* 30 (2): 345-74.

Burden, D. S. 1986. Single Parents and the work setting: The impact of multiple jobs and homelife responsibilities. *Family Relations* 35:37-43.

Buss, D. 1989. Sex differences in human mate preferences: Evolutionary hypotheses tests in 37 cultures. *Behavioral and Brain Sciences* 12:1-49.

Butler, Robert. 1975. *Why survive? Being old in America.* New York: Harper & Row.

Buunk, B. 1987. Conditions that promote breakups as a condition of extradyadic involvements. *Journal of Social and Clinical Psychology* 5 (3): 271-84.

Chaves, Mark. 1996. Ordaining women: The diffusion of an organizational innovation. *American Journal of Sociology* 101 (4): 840-73.

———. 1997. *Ordaining women: Culture and conflict in religious organizations.* Cambridge, MA: Harvard University Press.

Chen, Lucie, and Yen Espiritu. 1989. Korean businesses in black and Hispanic neighborhoods: A study of intergroup relations. *Sociological Perspectives* 32:521-34.

Cochran, Susan, and Vickie Mays. 1999. Sociocultural facets of the black gay male experience. In *The Black family: Essays and studies,* edited by Robert Staples, pp. 349-55. Belmont, CA: Wadsworth.

Collins, M. E. 1991. Body figure perceptions and preferences among pre-adolescent children. *International Journal of Eating Disorders* 199-208.

Collins, Patricia Hill. 2000. *Black feminist thought: Knowledge, consciousness, and the politics of empowerment.* New York: Routledge.

Comiskey, Andrew. 2003. *Strength in weakness: Healing sexual and relational brokenness.* Downers Grove, IL: InterVarsity Press.

Conroy, Hilary, and Harry Wray, eds. 1990. *Pearl Harbor reexamined: Prologue to the Pacific War.* Honolulu: University of Hawaii Press.

Cooley, Charles Horton. 1964. *Human nature and the social order.* New York: Schocken.

Crowder, Kyle, and Stewart Tolnay. 2000. A new marriage squeeze for black women. *Journal of Marriage and the Family* 62 (3): 792-808.

Crowther, J. R. Lilly, P. Crawford and K. Shepherd. 1992. The stability of the eating disorder inventory. *International Journal of Eating Disorders* 12 (1): 97-101.

Dash, Michael, Jonathan Jackson and Steve Rasor. 1997. *Hidden wholeness: An African-American spirituality for individuals and communities.* Cleveland: United Church Press.

Davies, Bob, and Lela Gilbert. 2001. *Portrait of freedom: 14 people who came out of homosexuality.* Downers Grove, IL: InterVarsity Press.

Deddo, Gary. 1997. Persons in racial reconciliation: The contributions of a trinitarian theological anthropology. In *The gospel in black & white: Theological resources for racial reconciliation,* edited by Dennis L. Okholm, pp. 58-70. Downers Grove, IL: InterVarsity Press.

Dennis, Everette E., and Edward C. Pease, eds. 1997. *The media in black and white.* New Brunswick, NJ: Transaction Publishers.

Dollard, John. 1939. *Frustration and aggression.* New Haven, CT: Yale University Press.

Drake, St. Clair, and Horace R. Cayton. [1945] 1962. *Black metropolis: A study of Negro life in a Northern City.* 2 vols. New York: Harper & Row.

Duckitt, John. 1992. *The social psychology of prejudice.* New York: Praeger.

Duncan, G., J. Boisjoly and T. Smeeding. 1996. Economic mobility of young workers in the 1970s and 1980s. *Demography* 33 (4): 497-509.

Duncan, O. 1979. How destination depends on origin in the occupational mobility table. *American Journal of Sociology* 84 (4): 793-803.

Eggebeen, David, and Daniel Lichter. 1991. Race, family structure and changing poverty among American children. *American Sociological Review* 56 (6): 801-17.

Espiritu, Yen Le. 1992. *Asian American panethnicity: Bridging institutions and identities.* Philadelphia: Temple University Press.

Etzioni, Amitai. 1991. Too many rights, too few responsibilities. *Society* 28 (2): 41-48.

Evans, Tony. 1995. *Let's get to know each other.* Nashville: Thomas Nelson.

Fairburn, C., R. Jones, R. Peveler, R. Hope and M. O'Connor. 1993. Psychotherapy and bulimia-nervosa: Longer-term effects of interpersonal psychotherapy, behavior-therapy, and cognitive-behavior therapy. *Archives of General Psychiatry* 50 (6): 419-28.

Feagin, Joe. 1975. *Subordinating the poor.* Englewood Cliffs, NJ: Prentice Hall.

———. 1991. The continuing significance of race: Antiblack discrimination in public places. *American Sociological Review* 56:101-16.

Ford, Clyde. 1994. *We can all get along: 50 steps you can take to help end racism.* New York: Dell Paperback.

Fossett, Mark, and K. Jill Kiecolt. 1989. The relative size of minority populations and white racial attitudes. *Social Science Quarterly* 70:820-35.

Franklin, Clyde W., and Walter Pillow. 1999. Single and married: The black male's acceptance of the prince charming ideal. In *The black family: Essays and studies,* edited by Robert Staples, pp. 87-93. Belmont, CA: Wadsworth.

Frazier, Sundee Tucker. 2001. *Check all that apply: Finding wholeness as a multiracial person.* Downers Grove, IL: InterVarsity Press.

Freud, Sigmund. 1960. *The ego and the id.* New York: W. W. Norton.

———. 1963. *General psychological theory.* New York: Colliers.

Funderburg, Lise. 1994. *Black, white, other: Biracial Americans talk about race and identity.* New York: W. Morrow.

Gallagher, Charles A., ed. 1999. *Rethinking the color line: Readings in race and ethnicity.* Mountain View, CA: Mayfield.

Gans, Herbert. 1994. Positive functions of the undeserving poor: Uses of the underclass in America. *Politics and Society* 22 (3): 269-83.

Gaertner, John, and Samuel Dovidio. 1986. *Prejudice, racism, and discrimination.* Orlando: Academic Press.

Goffman, Erving. 1959. *The presentation of self in everyday life.* New York: Anchor Books.

———. 1979. *Gender advertisements.* New York: Harper Colophon.

Granovetter, Mark. 1973. The strength of weak ties. *American Journal of Sociology* 78 (6): 1360-80.

———. 1993. The strength of weak ties: A network theory revisited. In *Sociology theory.* Stony Brook: State University of New York Press.

Grant, Donald. 1975. *The lynching movement.* San Francisco: R and E Research Associates.

Grant, Jacqueline. 1989. *White women's Christ and black women's Jesus: Feminist Christology and womanist response*. Atlanta: Scholars Press.

Green, D. P., D. Strolovitch, J. Wong and R. Bailey. 2001. Measuring gay populations and antigay hate crime. *Social Science Quarterly* 82 (2): 281-96.

Greer, Edward. 1979. *Black steel: Black politics and corporate power in Gary, Indiana*. New York: Monthly Review Press.

Griswold del Castillo, Richard, and Richard A. Garcia. 1995. *César Chávez: A triumph of spirit*. Norman: University of Oklahoma Press.

Haley, Alex. 1973. *The Autobiography of Malcolm X*. New York: Ballantine Books.

Hall, Walter Phelps. 1947. *World Wars and revolutions: The course of Europe since 1900*. New York: D. Appleton-Century.

Has Europe Come to America? *Gary American,* October 12, 1945, p. 4.

Hayes, Floyd W., ed. 2000. *A turbulent voyage: Readings in African American studies*. 3rd ed. San Diego: Collegiate Press.

Herek, G. M., J. Cogan and J. Gillis. 2002. Victim experiences in hate crimes based on sexual orientation. *Journal of Social Issues* 58 (2): 319-39.

Hewlett, Sylvia A. 1994. Public choices: Shortchanging the future. In *Contemporary societies: Problems and prospects,* ed. Daniel Curran and Claire Renzetti, pp. 260-68. Englewood Cliffs; NJ: Prentice Hall.

Hopson, Darlene, and Derek Hopson. 1993. *Raising the rainbow generation: Teaching your children to be successful in a multicultural society*. New York: Fireside Books.

Horowitz, Irving. 1993. *The decomposition of sociology*. New York: Oxford University Press.

Jackman, Mary. 1977. Prejudice, tolerance, and attitudes toward ethnic groups. *Social Science Research* 6:145-69.

Janis, Irving. 1972. *Victims of Groupthink*. Boston: Houghton Mifflin.

Jaret, Charles. 1994. *Poverty and place: Ghettos, barrios, and the American city*. New York: Russell Sage Foundation.

———. 1995. *Contemporary racial and ethnic relations*. New York: HarperCollins College.

Jargowsky, Paul A. 1994. *Poverty and Place: Ghettos, barrios, and the American city*. New York: Russell Sage Foundation.

______. 1996. Take the money and run: Economic segregation in U.S. metropolitan areas. *American Sociological Review* 61:984-998.

Jones, Stanton, and Mark Yarhouse. 2000. *Homosexuality: The use of scientific research in the church's moral debate*. Downers Grove, IL: InterVarsity Press.

Kane, R. J. 2003. Social control in the metropolis: A community-level examination of the minority group-threat hypothesis. *Justice Quarterly* 20 (2): 265-95.

Katz, D., and K. Braly. 1933. Racial stereotypes of 100 college students. *Journal of Abnormal and Social Psychology* 28:280-90.

Keener, Craig. 1997. The gospel and racial reconciliation. In *The gospel in black & white: Theological resources for racial reconciliation,* edited by Dennis L. Okholm, pp. 117-30. Downers Grove, IL: InterVarsity Press.

King, Mary. 1992. Occupational segregation by race and sex, 1940-1988. *Monthly Labor Review* 30-37.

Kirschenman, Joleen and Kathryn Neckerman. 1991. "We'd love to hire them, but . . .": The meaning of race for employers. *Social Problems* 38 (4): 433-47.

Kohlberg, Lawrence. 1981. *The psychology of moral development: The nature and validity of moral stages*. New York: Harper & Row.

Konieczny, Mary, and Mark Chaves. 2000. Resources, race, and female-headed congregations in the United States. *Journal for the Scientific Study of Religion* 39 (3): 261-71.

Kunovich, R. M. 2004. Social structural position and prejudice: An exploration of cross-national differences in regression slopes. *Social Science Research* 33 (1): 20-44.

Lee, John A. 1974. The method of measuring love. *Psychology Today* 8:43-51.

———. 1977. A typology of styles of loving. *Personality and Social Psychology Bulletin* 3:173-82.

Leland, John, and Mark Miller. 1998. Can gays convert? *Newsweek,* August 17, pp. 47-53.

Levin, B. 2002. From slavery to hate crime laws: The emergence of race and status-based protection in American criminal law. *Journal of Social Issues* 58 (2): 227-45.

Lincoln, C. Eric, and Lawrence H. Mamiya. 1990. *The black church in the African-American experience*. Durham, NC: Duke University Press.

MacDonald, Fred. 1992. *Black and White TV: African Americans in television since 1948*. Chicago: Nelsen-Hall.

Macionis, John J. 1999. *Sociology*. 7th ed. Englewood Cliffs, NJ: Prentice Hall.

MacLeod, Jay. 1995. *Ain't no makin' it*. Boulder, CO: Westview Press.

Marx, Karl. [1848] 1977. *The Marx-Engels Reader,* edited by Robert C. Tucker. New York: Norton.

Maslov, Abraham. 1954. *Motivation and personality*. New York: Harper.

Massey, Douglas S., and Nancy A. Denton. 1993. *American apartheid: Segregation and the making of the underclass*. Cambridge, MA: Harvard University Press.

Mays, Vickie, and Susan Cochran. 1999. The black woman's relationship project: A national survey on black lesbians. In *The black family: Essays and studies,* edited by Robert Staples, pp. 59-69. Belmont, CA: Wadsworth.

McConahay, John. 1983. Modern racism and modern discrimination: The effects of race, racial-attitudes, and context on simulated hiring decisions. *Personality and Social Psychology Bulletin* 9 (4): 551-58.

McCormick, Naomi, and Clinton Jesser. 1988. The courtship game. In *Family re-*

lations: A reader, edited by Norval Glenn and Marion Coleman. Chicago: Dorsey Press.

McCullough, Michael E., Steven Sandage and Everett Worthington. 1997. *To forgive is human: How to put your past in the past.* Downers Grove, IL: InterVarsity Press.

McRae, Susan. 1986. *Cross-class families: A study of wives' occupational superiority.* New York: Oxford University Press.

McRoberts, Omar M. 2003. *Streets of glory: Church and community in a black urban neighborhood.* Chicago: University of Chicago Press.

Mead, George Herbert. 1962. *Mind, self, and society.* Chicago: University of Chicago Press.

Mellin, L. S. McNutt, Y. Hu, G. Schreiber, P. Crawford and E. Obarzanek. 1991. A Longitudinal study of the dietary practices of black and white girls 9 and 10 years old at enrollment: The NHBLBI growth and health study. *Journal of Adolescent Health* 27-37.

Merton, Robert. 1968. *Social theory and social structure.* New York: Free Press.

Mitchell, J. Paul. 1970. *Race riots in black and white.* Englewood Cliffs, NJ: Prentice-Hall.

Mohl, Raymond, and Neil Benton. 1986. *Steel city: Urban and ethnic patterns in Gary, Indiana, 1906-1950.* New York: Holmes & Meier.

Morris, Aldon D. 1984. *The origins of the Civil Rights Movement: Black communities organizing for change.* New York: Free Press.

Myrdal, Gunnar. 1962. *An American dilemma: The Negro problem and modern democracy.* New York: Harper & Row.

Nagel, J. 1994. Constructing ethnicity: Creating and recreating ethnic-identity and culture. *Social Problems* 41 (1): 152-76.

Newman, Katherine S. 1988. *Falling from grace: Downward mobility in the age of affluence.* Berkeley: University of California Press.

———. 1993. *Declining fortunes: The withering of the American dream.* New York: Basic Books.

———. 1999. *No shame in my game: The working poor in the inner city.* New York: Alfred A. Knopf and The Russell Sage Foundation.

Nolan, J. J., Y. Akuyama and S. Berhanu. 2002. The Hate crime statistics act of 1990: Developing a method for measuring the occurrence of hate violence. *American Behavioral Scientist* 46 (1): 136-53.

NORC. 1994. *General social surveys, 1972-1994: Cumulative codebook.* University of Chicago: National Opinion Research.

———. 1996. *General social surveys, 1972-1996: Cumulative codebook.* Chicago: National Opinion Research.

Nouwen, Henry. 1989. *Lifesigns: Intimacy, fecundity, and ecstasy in Christian perspective.* New York: Crossroad.

O'Hare, William, Willam Frey and Dan Fost. 1994. Asians in the suburbs. *Amer-*

ican Demographics 16 (9): 32-38.

Okholm, Dennis L., ed. 1997. *The gospel in black & white: Theological resources for racial reconciliation.* Downers Grove, IL: InterVarsity Press.

Omi, Michael and Howard Winant. 1994. *Racial formation in the United States: From the 1960s to the 1990s.* New York: Routledge.

Ortiz, Vilma. 1991. Women of color: A demographic overview. In *Women of color in US society,* edited by Maxine Zinn and Bonnie Dill, pp. 13-32. Philadelphia: Temple University Press.

Pearce, Diana M. 1983. The Feminization of ghetto poverty. *Society* 21 (1): 70-74.

Pennebaker, James, Cheryl Hughes and Robin O'Heeron. 1987. The psychophysiology of confession: Linking inhibitory and psychosomatic processes. *Journal of Personality and Social Psychology* 52:781-93.

Perkins, Spencer, and Chris Rice. 2000. *More than equals: Racial healing for the sake of the gospel.* Downers Grove, IL: InterVarsity Press.

Perry, B. 2002. Defending the color line: Racially and ethnically motivated hate crime. *American Behavioral Scientist* 46 (1): 72-92.

Piaget, J. 1951. *Play, dreams, and imitation in children.* New York: Norton.

Quarles, Benjamin. 1987. *The Negro in the making of America.* New York: Collier.

Rayburn, N. R., M. Earleywine and G. C. Davison. 2003. Base rates of hate crime victimization among college students. *Journal of Interpersonal Violence* 18 (10): 1209-21.

Rippe, J. M. 1996. Overweight and health: Communications, challenges, and opportunities. *American Journal of Clinical Nutrition* 63 (3): 470-73.

Roedinger, David R. 1991. *The wages of whiteness: Race and the making of the American working class.* London: Verso.

Roth, G., and C. Wittich, eds. 1978. *Economy and society.* Berkeley: University of California Press.

Russell, Bob. 2004. *The power of one another: Developing Christian relationships.* Cincinnati: Standard Publishing.

Russell, Kathy, Midge Wilson and Ronald Hall. 1992. *The color complex: The politics of skin color among African Americans.* New York: Harcourt Brace Jovanovich.

Samuelson, Robert. 1988. The elderly aren't needy. *Newsweek,* March 21, p. 68.

Schuller, Robert. 1993. *Power thoughts.* New York: Harper Collins.

Schuman, Howard, and Jacqueline Scott. 1989. Generations and collective memories. *American Sociological Review* 30:843-61.

Scott, J. Julius. 1997. Acts 10:34, a text for racial and cultural reconciliation among Christians. In *The gospel in black & white: Theological resources for racial reconciliation,* edited by Dennis L. Okholm, pp. 131-42. Downers Grove, IL: InterVarsity Press.

Seals, D., and J. Young. 2003. Bullying and victimization: Prevalence and relationship to gender, grade level, ethnicity, self-esteem, and depression. *Adolescence* 38 (152): 735-47.

Shapiro, Fred C., and James W. Sullivan. 1964. *Race riots.* New York: Crowell.

Sharp, Douglas. 2002. *No partiality: The idolatry of race and the new humanity.* Downers Grove, IL: InterVarsity Press.

Sittser, Gerald. 1994. *Loving across our differences.* Downers Grove, IL: InterVarsity Press.

Sjostrom, Lisa. 1996. *Bullyproof: A teacher's guide on teasing and bullying: For use with fourth and fifth grade students.* Wellesley, MA: Wellesley College Center for Research on Women and the NEA Professional Library.

Smedley, J. W., and J. A. Bayton. 1978. Evaluative race-class stereotypes by race and perceived class of subjects. *Journal of Personality and Social Psychology* 36:530-35.

Smith, Tom. 1996. Anti-Semitism decreases but persists. *Society* 33 (3): 2.

Sorensen, J., R. Hope and D. Stemen. 2003. Racial disproportionality in state prison admissions: Can regional variation be explained by differential arrest rates? *Journal of Criminal Justice* 31 (1): 73-84.

Staples, Robert. 1999a. *The black family: Essays and studies.* Belmont, CA: Wadsworth.

———. 1999b. Interracial relationships: A convergence of desire and opportunity. In *The black family: Essays and studies,* ed. Robert Staples, pp. 129-36. Belmont, CA: Wadsworth.

Stassen, Glen, and David Gushee. 2003. *Kingdom ethics: Following Jesus in contemporary context.* Downers Grove, IL: InterVarsity Press.

Steinberg, A., J. Brooks and T. Remtulla. 2003. Youth hate crimes: Identification, prevention, and intervention. *American Journal of Psychiatry* 160 (5): 979-89.

Stones, Rosemary. 1993. *Don't pick on me: How to handle bullying.* Markham, Ontario: Pembroke.

Tajfel, Henri. 1982. Social psychology of intergroup relations. *Annual Review of Psychology,* pp. 1-39.

Tanhill, R. 1980. *Sex in history.* New York: Stein & Day.

Tatum, Beverly. 1999. *Why are all the black kids sitting together in the cafeteria? And other conversations about race.* New York: Basic Books.

Taylor, John. 1991. Don't blame me: The new culture of victimization. *New York Magazine,* June 3, pp. 26-34.

Thompson, Becky. 2002. Eating problems among African American, Latina, and white women. In *Contemporary ethnic families in the U.S.: characteristics, variations, and dynamics,* ed. Nijole Benekraitis, pp. 279-88. Englewood Cliffs, NJ: Prentice Hall.

Tienda, Marta, Katharine Donato and Hector Cordero-Guzman. 1992. Schooling, color, and labor force activity of women. *Social Forces* 71: 365-395.

Townsend-Gilkes. 2001. *If it wasn't for the women: Black women's experience and womanist culture in church and community.* Maryknoll, NY: Orbis.

Tucker, Cynthia. 1996. Women and the Unitarian-Universalist ministry. In *Reli-*

gious institutions and women's leadership, edited by Catherine Wessinger. Columbia: University of South Carolina Press.

Tucker, M. Belinda, and Claudia Mitchell-Kernan. 1990. New trends in black Americans' interracial marriage: The social structural context. *Journal of Marriage and the Family* 52:207-18.

U.S. Bureau of the Census. 2004. *Income, poverty, and health insurance coverage in the United States: 2003.* Washington, DC: U.S. Government Printing Office.

Veblen, Thorstein. 1953. *The theory of the leisure class.* New York: New American Library.

Wachs, Faye, and Shari Dworkin. 1997. There's no such thing as a gay hero. *Journal of Sport & Social Issues* 21 (4): 327-47.

Washington, Raleigh, and Glen Kehrein. 1996. *Breaking down walls: A model for reconciliation in an age of racial strife.* Chicago: Moody Press.

Waters, Mary C. 1999. Ethnic and racial identities of second-generation black immigrants in New York city. In *Rethinking the color line: Readings in race and ethnicity,* edited by Charles A. Gallagher, pp. 421-36. Mountain View, CA: Mayfield.

Weber, Max. [1921] 1978. *Economy and society,* edited by G. Roth and C. Wittich. Berkeley: University of California Press.

Webster-Doyle, Terrence. 1991. *Why is everybody always picking on me? A guide to understanding bullies for young people.* Middlebury, VT: Atrium Society.

Webster's Ninth New Collegiate Dictionary. 1986. Springfield, MA: Merriam-Webster.

Weitzman, Lenore. 1985. *The divorce revolution: The unexpected social and economic consequences for women and children in America.* New York: Free Press.

Wellman, N. S., and B. Friedberg. 2002. Causes and consequences of adult obesity: Health, social and economic impacts in the United States. *Asia Pacific Journal of Clinical Nutrition* 11:705-9.

Wells-Barnett, Ida. 1969. *On lynchings: Southern horrors, a red record, mob rule in New Orleans.* New York: Arno Press.

———. 1970. *Crusade for justice: The autobiography of Ida B. Wells.* Chicago: University of Chicago Press.

Wessinger, Catherine, ed. 1996. *Religious institutions and women's leadership.* Columbia: University of South Carolina Press.

West, Cornel. 1993. *Race matters.* Boston: Beacon.

Wilmore, Gayraud S., ed. 1994. *Black religion and black radicalism: An interpretation of the religious history of Afro-American people.* New York: Orbis.

———. 1995. *African-American religious studies: An interdisciplinary anthology.* Durham, NC: Duke University Press.

Wilmore, David. 1995. The manhood puzzle. In *Manhood in the making,* edited by David Gilmore, pp. 9-29. New Haven, Conn.: Yale University Press.

Wilson, S., and N. Medora. 1990. Gender comparisons of college students' attitudes toward sexual behavior. *Adolescence* 25:615-27.

Wilson, William Julius. 1987. *The truly disadvantaged: The inner city, the underclass, and public policy*. Chicago: University of Chicago Press.

———. 1996. *When work disappears: The world of the new urban poor.* New York: Alfred A. Knopf.

Wimberly, Anne Streaty. 1994. Soul stories: African American christian education. Nashville: Abingdon Press.

Wolf, Naomi. 1991. *The beauty myth: How images of beauty are used against women*. New York: W. Morris.

Wright, Jeremiah A., Jr. 1993. *What makes you so strong? Sermons of joy and strength*. Valley Forge, PA: Judson Press.

Zangwill, Israel. 1921. *The melting pot*. New York: Macmillan.

Zhou, Min. 1992. *Chinatown: The socioeconomic potential of an urban enclave.* Philadelphia: Temple University Press.

Names Index

Subject Index

Scripture Index